𝔖𝔱𝔞𝔫𝔡𝔞𝔯𝔡 𝔏𝔦𝔟𝔯𝔞𝔯𝔶 𝔈𝔡𝔦𝔱𝔦𝔬𝔫

AMERICAN STATESMEN

EDITED BY

JOHN T. MORSE, JR.

IN THIRTY-TWO VOLUMES

VOL. XV.

THE JEFFERSONIAN DEMOCRACY
JOHN QUINCY ADAMS

John Quincy Adams

American Statesmen

STANDARD LIBRARY EDITION

The Home of John Quincy Adams

HOUGHTON, MIFFLIN & CO.

American Statesmen

JOHN QUINCY ADAMS

BY

JOHN T. MORSE, JR.

BOSTON AND NEW YORK
HOUGHTON, MIFFLIN AND COMPANY
The Riverside Press, Cambridge

PREFACE

NEARLY sixteen years have elapsed since this book was written. In that time sundry inaccuracies have been called to my attention, and have been corrected, and it may be fairly hoped that after the lapse of so long a period all errors in matters of fact have been eliminated. I am not aware that any fresh material has been made public, or that any new views have been presented which would properly lead to alterations in the substance of what is herein said. If I were now writing the book for the first time, I should do what so many of the later contributors to the series have very wisely and advantageously done : I should demand more space. But this was the first volume published, and at a time when the enterprise was still an experiment insistence upon such a point, especially on the part of the editor, would have been unreasonable. Thus it happens that, though Mr. Adams was appointed minister resident at the Hague in 1794, and thereafter continued in public life, almost without interruption, until

his death in February, 1848, the narrative of
his career is compressed within little more than
three hundred pages. The proper function of
a work upon this scale is to draw a picture of
the man.

With the picture which I have drawn of Mr.
Adams, I still remain moderately contented —
by which remark I mean nothing more egotistical than that I believe it to be a correct picture,
and done with whatever measure of skill I may
happen to possess in portraiture. I should like
to change it only in one particular, viz. : by in-
fusing throughout the volume somewhat more
of admiration. Adams has never received the
praise which was his due, and probably he never
will receive it. In order that justice should be
done him by the public, his biographer ought
to speak somewhat better of him than his real
deserts would require. He presents one of those
cases where exaggeration is the servant of truth ;
for this moderate excess of appreciation would
only offset that discount from an accurate estimate which his personal unpopularity always has
caused, and probably always will cause, to be
made. He was a good instance of the rule that
the world will for the most part treat the individual as the individual treats the world. Adams
was censorious, not to say uncharitable in the

extreme, always in an attitude of antagonism,
always unsparing and denunciatory. The measure which he meted has been by others in their
turn meted to him. This habit of ungracious
criticism was his great fault; perhaps it was
almost his only very serious fault; it cost him
dear in his life, and has continued to cost his
memory dear since his death. Sometimes we
are not sorry to see men get the punishments
which they have brought on themselves; yet we
ought to be sorry for Mr. Adams. After all,
his fault-finding was in part the result of his
respect for virtue and his hatred of all that was
ignoble and unworthy. If he despised a low
standard, at least he held his own standard
high, and himself lived by the rules by which
he measured others. Men with vastly greater
defects have been much more kindly served both
by contemporaries and by posterity. There can
be no question that Adams deserved all the
esteem which ought to be accorded to the highest moral qualities, to very high, if a little short
of the highest, intellectual endowment, and to
immense acquirements. His political integrity
was of a grade rarely seen; and, in unison with
his extraordinary courage and independence, it
seemed to the average politician actually irritating and offensive. He was in the same difficulty

in which Aristides the Just found himself. But
neither assaults nor political solitude daunted or
discouraged him. His career in the House of
Representatives is a tale which has not a rival
in congressional history. I regret that it could
not be told here at greater length. Stubbornly
fighting for freedom of speech and against the
slaveholders, fierce and unwearied in old age,
falling literally out of the midst of the conflict
into his grave, Mr. Adams, during the closing
years of his life, is one of the most striking
figures of modern times. I beg the reader of
this volume to put into its pages more warmth
of praise than he will find therein, and so do
a more correct justice to an honest statesman
and a gallant friend of the oppressed. Doing
this, he will improve my book in the particular
wherein I think that it chiefly needs improvement.

JOHN T. MORSE, JR.

July, 1898.

CONTENTS

CHAPTER I.

ILLUSTRATIONS

JOHN QUINCY ADAMS

CHAPTER I

YOUTH AND DIPLOMACY

On July 11, 1767, in the North Parish of Braintree, since set off as the town of Quincy, in Massachusetts, was born John Quincy Adams. Two streams of as good blood as flowed in the colony mingled in the veins of the infant. If heredity counts for anything he began life with an excellent chance of becoming famous — *non sine dîs animosus infans*. He was called after his great-grandfather on the mother's side, John Quincy, a man of local note who had borne in his day a distinguished part in provincial affairs. Such a naming was a simple and natural occurrence enough, but Mr. Adams afterward moralized upon it in his characteristic way: —

"The incident which gave rise to this circumstance is not without its moral to my heart. He was dying when I was baptized ; and his daughter, my grandmother, present at my birth, requested that I might

receive his name. The fact, recorded by my father
at the time, has connected with that portion of my
name a charm of mingled sensibility and devotion.
It was filial tenderness that gave the name. It was
the name of one passing from earth to immortality.
These have been among the strongest links of my
attachment to the name of Quincy, and have been to
me through life a perpetual admonition to do nothing
unworthy of it."

Fate, which had made such good preparation
for him before his birth, was not less kind in
arranging the circumstances of his early training and development. His father was deeply
engaged in the patriot cause, and the first
matters borne in upon his opening intelligence
concerned the public discontent and resistance
to tyranny. He was but seven years old when
he clambered with his mother to the top of one
of the high hills in the neighborhood of his
home to listen to the sounds of conflict upon
Bunker's Hill, and to watch the flaming ruin
of Charlestown. Profound was the impression
made upon him by the spectacle, and it was
intensified by many an hour spent afterward
upon the same spot during the siege and bom-
bardment of Boston. Then John Adams went
as a delegate to the Continental Congress at
Philadelphia, and his wife and children were
left for twelve months, as John Quincy Adams

says, — it is to be hoped with a little exaggeration of the barbarity of British troops toward women and babes. — "liable every hour of the day and of the night to be butchered in cold blood, or taken and carried into Boston as hostages, by any foraging or marauding detachment." Later, when the British had evacuated Boston, the boy, barely nine years old, became "post-rider" between the city and the farm, a distance of eleven miles each way, in order to bring all the latest news to his mother.

Not much regular schooling was to be got amid such surroundings of times and events, but the lad had a natural aptitude or affinity for knowledge which stood him in better stead than could any dame of a village school. The following letter to his father is worth preserving: —

BRAINTREE, *June the 2d*, 1777.

DEAR SIR, — I love to receive letters very well, much better than I love to write them. I make but a poor figure at composition, my head is much too fickle, my thoughts are running after birds' eggs, play and trifles till I get vexed with myself. I have but just entered the 3d volume of Smollett, tho' I had designed to have got it half through by this time. I have determined this week to be more diligent, as Mr. Thaxter will be absent at Court and I Cannot pursue my other Studies. I have Set myself a Stent and determine to read the 3d volume Half out. If

I can but keep my resolution I will write again at the end of the week and give a better account of myself. I wish, Sir, you would give me some instructions with regard to my time, and advise me how to proportion my Studies and my Play, in writing, and I will keep them by me and endeavor to follow them. I am, dear Sir, with a present determination of growing better. Yours.

P. S. Sir, if you will be so good as to favor me with a Blank book, I will transcribe the most remarkable occurrences I mett with in my reading, which will serve to fix them upon my mind.

Not long after the writing of this model epistle, the simple village life was interrupted by an unexpected change. John Adams was sent on a diplomatic journey to Paris, and on February 13, 1778, embarked in the frigate Boston. John Quincy Adams, then eleven years old, accompanied his father and thus made his first acquaintance with the foreign lands where so many of his coming years were to be passed. This initial visit, however, was brief; and he was hardly well established at school when events caused his father to start for home. Unfortunately this return trip was a needless loss of time, since within three months of their setting foot upon American shores the two travellers were again on their stormy way back across the Atlantic in a leaky ship, which had to land them at the nearest port in Spain. One more quotation must be given from a letter written just after the first arrival in France : —

PASSY, *September the 27th*, 1778.

HONORED MAMMA, — My Pappa enjoins it upon me to keep a Journal, or a Diary of the Events that happen to me, and of objects that I see, and of Characters that I converse with from day to day; and altho' I am Convinced of the utility, importance and necessity of this Exercise, yet I have not patience and perseverance enough to do it so Constantly as I ought. My Pappa, who takes a great deal of pains to put me in the right way, has also advised me to Preserve Copies of all my letters, and has given me a Convenient Blank Book for this end; and altho' I shall have the mortification a few years hence to read a great deal of my Childish nonsense, yet I shall have the Pleasure and advantage of Remarking the several steps by which I shall have advanced in taste, judgment and knowledge. A Journal Book and a letter Book of a Lad of Eleven years old Can not be expected to Contain much of Science, Literature, arts, wisdom, or wit, yet it may serve to perpetuate many observations that I may make, and may hereafter help me to recollect both persons and things that would other ways escape my memory.

He continues with resolutions "to be more thoughtful and industrious for the future," and reflects with pleasure upon the prospect that

his scheme " will be a sure means of improvement to myself, and enable me to be more entertaining to you." What gratification must
this letter from one who was quite justified in
signing himself her " dutiful and affectionate
son " have brought to the Puritan bosom of the
good mother at home! If the plan for the diary
was not pursued during the first short flitting
abroad, it can hardly be laid at the door of the
" lad of eleven years " as a serious fault. He
did in fact begin it when setting out on the
aforementioned second trip to Europe, calling it

A JOURNAL BY J. Q. A.,

From America to Spain.

Vol. I.

Begun Friday, 12 of November, 1779.

The spark of life in the great undertaking
flickered in a somewhat feeble and irregular
way for many years thereafter, but apparently
gained strength by degrees until in 1795, as
Mr. C. F. Adams tells us, " what may be de-
nominated the diary proper begins," a very
vigorous work in more senses than one. Continued with astonishing persistency and faithfulness until within a few days of the writer's
death, the latest entry is of the 4th of January,
1848. Mr. Adams achieved many successes

during his life as the result of conscious effort, but the greatest success of all he achieved altogether unconsciously. He left a portrait of himself more full, correct, vivid, and picturesque than has ever been bequeathed to posterity by any other personage of the past ages. Any mistakes which may be made in estimating his mental or moral attributes must be charged to the dulness or prejudice of the judge, who could certainly not ask for better or more abundant evidence. Few of us know our most intimate friends better than any of us may know Mr. Adams, if we will but take the trouble. Even the brief extracts already given from his correspondence show us the boy; it only concerns us to get them into the proper light for seeing them accurately. If a lad of seven, nine, or eleven years of age should write such solemn little effusions amid the surroundings and influences of the present day, he would probably be set down justly enough as either an offensive young prig or a prematurely developed hypocrite. But the precocious Adams had only a little of the prig and nothing of the hypocrite in his nature. Being the outcome of many generations of simple, devout, intelligent Puritan ancestors, living in a community which loved virtue and sought knowledge, all inherited and all present influences

combined to make him, as it may be put in a
single word, sensible. He had inevitably a
mental boyhood and youth, but morally he was
never either a child or a lad; all his leading
traits of character were as strongly marked
when he was seven as when he was seventy,
and at an age when most young people simply
win love or cause annoyance, he was preferring
wisdom to mischief, and actually in his earliest
years was attracting a certain respect.

These few but bold and striking touches
which paint the boy are changed for an infinitely more elaborate and complex presentation
from the time when the Diary begins. Even
as abridged in the printing, this immense work
ranks among the half-dozen longest diaries to
be found in any library, and it is unquestionably by far the most valuable. Henceforth we
are to travel along its broad route to the end;
we shall see in it both the great and the small
among public men halting onward in a way
very different from that in which they march
along the stately pages of the historian, and we
shall find many side-lights, by no means color-
less, thrown upon the persons and events of the
procession. The persistence, fulness, and faithfulness with which it was kept throughout so
busy a life are marvellous, but are also highly
characteristic of the most persevering and in-

dustrious of men. That it has been preserved is cause not only for thankfulness but for some surprise also. For if its contents had been known, it is certain that all the public men of nearly two generations who figure in it would have combined into one vast and irresistible conspiracy to obtain and destroy it. There was always a superfluity of gall in the diarist's ink. Sooner or later every man of any note in the United States was mentioned in his pages, and there is scarcely one of them, who, if he could have read what was said of him, would not have preferred the ignominy of omission. As one turns the leaves he feels as though he were walking through a graveyard of slaughtered reputations wherein not many headstones show a few words of measured commendation. It is only the greatness and goodness of Mr. Adams himself which relieve the universal atmosphere of sadness far more depressing than the melancholy which pervades the novels of George Eliot. The reader who wishes to retain any comfortable degree of belief in his fellow men will turn to the wall all the portraits in the gallery except only the inimitable one of the writer himself. For it would be altogether too discouraging to think that so wide an experience of men as Mr. Adams enjoyed through his long, varied, and active life must lead to such an unpleasant ar-

ray of human faces as those which are scattered
along these twelve big octavos. Fortunately at
present we have to do with only one of these
likenesses, and that one we are able to admire
while knowing also that it is beyond question
accurate. One after another every trait of Mr.
Adams comes out; we shall see that he was a
man of a very high and noble character veined
with some very notable and disagreeable blem-
ishes; his aspirations were honorable, even the
lowest of them being more than simply respectable; he had an avowed ambition, but it was of
that pure kind which led him to render true
and distinguished services to his countrymen;
he was not only a zealous patriot, but a profound
believer in the sound and practicable tenets of
the liberal political creed of the United States;
he had one of the most honest and independent
natures that was ever given to man; personal
integrity of course goes without saying, but he
had the rarer gift of an elevated and rigid political honesty such as has been unfrequently seen
in any age or any nation; in times of severe
trial this quality was even cruelly tested, but we
shall never see it fail; he was as courageous as
if he had been a fanatic; indeed, for a long part
of his life to maintain a single-handed fight in
support of a despised or unpopular opinion
seemed his natural function and almost exclu-

sive calling; he was thoroughly conscientious and never knowingly did wrong, nor even sought to persuade himself that wrong was right; well read in literature and of wide and varied information in nearly all matters of knowledge, he was more especially remarkable for his acquirements in the domain of politics, where indeed they were vast and ever growing; he had a clear and generally a cool head, and was nearly always able to do full justice to himself and to his cause; he had an indomitable will, unconquerable persistence, and infinite laboriousness. Such were the qualities which made him a great statesman; but unfortunately we must behold a hardly less striking reverse to the picture, in the faults and shortcomings which made him so unpopular in his lifetime that posterity is only just beginning to forget the prejudices of his contemporaries and to render concerning him the judgment which he deserves. Never did a man of pure life and just purposes have fewer friends or more enemies than John Quincy Adams. His nature, said to have been very affectionate in his family relations, was in its aspect outside of that small circle singularly cold and repellent. If he could ever have gathered even a small personal following his character and abilities would have insured him a brilliant and prolonged success; but, for a man of his calibre and influence, we shall see him as one of the most lonely and desolate of the great men of history; instinct led the public men of his time to range themselves against him rather than with him, and we shall find them fighting beside him only when irresistibly compelled to do so by policy or strong convictions. As he had little sympathy with those with whom he was brought in contact, so he was very uncharitable in his judgment of them; and thus having really a low opinion of so many of them he could indulge his vindictive rancor without stint; his invective, always powerful, will sometimes startle us by its venom, and we shall be pained to see him apt to make enemies for a good cause by making them for himself.

This has been, perhaps, too long a lingering upon the threshold. But Mr. Adams's career in public life stretched over so long a period that to write a full historical memoir of him within the limited space of this volume is impossible. All that can be attempted is to present a sketch of the man with a few of his more prominent surroundings against a very meagre and insufficient background of the history of the times. So it may be permissible to begin with a general outline of his figure, to be filled in, shaded, and colored as we proceed. At best our task is much more difficult of satisfactory

achievement that an historical biography of the
customary elaborate order.

During his second visit to Europe, our mature
youngster — if the word may be used of Mr.
Adams even in his earliest years — began to
see a good deal of the world and to mingle in
very distinguished society.   For a brief period
he got a little schooling, first at Paris, next at
Amsterdam, and then at Leyden ; altogether
the amount was insignificant, since he was not
quite fourteen years old when he actually found
himself engaged in a diplomatic career.   Francis
Dana, afterward Chief Justice of Massachusetts,
was then accredited as an envoy to Russia from
the United States. and he took Mr. Adams with
him as his private secretary.   Not much came
of the mission, but it was a valuable experience
for a lad of his years.   Upon his return he
spent six months in travel and then he rejoined
his father in Paris, where that gentleman was
engaged with Franklin and John Jay in negotiating the final treaty of peace between the
revolted colonies and the mother country.   The
boy " was at once enlisted in the service as
an additional secretary, and gave his help to
the preparation of the papers necessary to the
completion of that instrument which dispersed
all possible doubt of the Independence of his
Country."

On April 26, 1785, arrived the packet-ship
Le Courier de L'Orient, bringing a letter from
Mr. Gerry containing news of the appointment
of John Adams as Minister to St. James's. This
unforeseen occurrence made it necessary for the
younger Adams to determine his own career,
which apparently he was left to do for himself.
He was indeed a singular young man, not unworthy of such confidence ! The glimpses which
we get of him during this stay abroad show him
as the associate upon terms of equality with
grown men of marked ability and exercising
important functions. He preferred diplomacy
to dissipation, statesmen to mistresses, and in
the midst of all the temptations of the gayest
capital in the world, the chariness with which
he sprinkled his wild oats amid the alluring
gardens chiefly devoted to the culture of those
cereals might well have brought a blush to the
cheeks of some among his elders, at least if the
tongue of slander wags not with gross untruth
concerning the colleagues of John Adams.   But
he was not in Europe to amuse himself, though
at an age when amusement is natural and a
tinge of sinfulness is so often pardoned ; he was
there with the definite and persistent purpose
of steady improvement and acquisition. At his
age most young men play the cards which a
kind fortune puts into their hands, with the

reckless intent only of immediate gain, but from the earliest moment when he began the game of life Adams coolly and wisely husbanded every card which came into his hand, with a steady view to probable future contingencies, and with the resolve to win in the long run. So now the resolution which he took in the present question illustrated the clearness of his mind and the strength of his character. To go with his father to England would be to enjoy a life precisely fitted to his natural and acquired tastes, to mingle with the men who were making history, to be cognizant of the weightiest of public affairs, to profit by all that the grandest city in the world had to show. It was easy to be not only allured by the prospect but also to be deceived by its apparent advantages. Adams, however, had the sense and courage to turn his back on it, and to go home to the meagre shores and small society of New England, there to become a boy again, to enter Harvard College, and come under all its at that time rigid and petty regulations. It almost seems a mistake, but it was not. Already he was too ripe and too wise to blunder. He himself gives us his characteristic and sufficient reasons : —

"Were I now to go with my father probably my immediate satisfaction might be greater than it will

be in returning to America. After having been
travelling for these seven years almost and all over
Europe, and having been in the world and among
company for three; to return to spend one or two
years in the pale of a college, subjected to all the
rules which I have so long been freed from; and
afterwards not expect (however good an opinion I
may have of myself) to bring myself into notice
under three or four years more, if ever! It is really
a prospect somewhat discouraging for a youth of my
ambition, (for I have ambition though I hope its object is laudable). But still

'Oh! how wretched
Is that poor man, that hangs on Princes' favors,'

or on those of any body else. I am determined that
so long as I shall be able to get my own living in an
honorable manner, I will depend upon no one. My
father has been so much taken up all his lifetime
with the interests of the public, that his own fortune
has suffered by it: so that his children will have to
provide for themselves, which I shall never be able
to do if I loiter away my precious time in Europe
and shun going home until I am forced to it. With
an ordinary share of common sense, which I hope I
enjoy, at least in America I can live *independent* and
free; and rather than live otherwise I would wish to
die before the time when I shall be left at my own
discretion. I have before me a striking example of
the distressing and humiliating situation a person is
reduced to by adopting a different line of conduct,
and I am determined not to fall into the same error."

It is needless to comment upon such spirit and sense, or upon such just appreciation of what was feasible. wise, and right for him, as a New Englander whose surroundings and pro-, spects were widely different from those of the society about him. He must have been strongly imbued by nature with the instincts of his birth-place to have formed, after a seven years' absence at his impressible age, so correct a judgment of the necessities and possibilities of his own career in relationship to the people and ideas of his own country.

Home accordingly he came, and by assiduity prepared himself in a very short time to enter the junior class at Harvard College, whence he was graduated in high standing in 1787. From there he went to Newburyport, then a thriving and active seaport enriched by the noble trade of privateering in addition to more regular maritime business, and entered as a law student the office of Theophilus Parsons, afterwards the Chief Justice of Massachusetts. On July 15, 1790, being twenty-three years old, he was admitted to practice. Immediately afterward he established himself in Boston, where for a time he felt strangely solitary. Clients of course did not besiege his doors in the first year, and he appears to have waited rather stubbornly than cheerfully for more active days. These came in good time, and during the second, third, and fourth years, his business grew apace to encouraging dimensions.

He was, however, doing other work than that of the law, and much more important in its bearing upon his future career. He could not keep his thoughts, nor indeed his hands, from public affairs. When, in 1791, Thomas Paine produced the " Rights of Man," Thomas Jefferson acting as midwife to usher the bantling before the people of the United States, Adams's indignation was fired, and he published anonymously a series of refuting papers over the signature of Publicola. These attracted much attention, not only at home but also abroad, and were by many attributed to John Adams. Two years later, during the excitement aroused by the reception and subsequent outrageous behavior here of the French minister, Genet, Mr. Adams again published in the Boston " Centinel " some papers over the signature of Marcellus, discussing with much ability the then new and perplexing question of the neutrality which should be observed by this country in European wars. These were followed by more, over the signature of Columbus, and afterward by still more in the name of Barnevelt, all strongly reprobating the course of the crazy-headed foreigner. The writer was not

permitted to remain long unknown. It is not
certain, but it is highly probable, that to these
articles was due the nomination which Mr.
Adams received shortly afterward from President Washington, as Minister Resident at the
Hague. This nomination was sent in to the
Senate, May 29, 1794, and was unanimously
confirmed on the following day. It may be
imagined that the change from the moderate
practice of his Boston law office to a European
court, of which he so well knew the charms,
was not distasteful to him. There are passages in his Diary which indicate that he had
been chafing with irrepressible impatience " in
that state of useless and disgraceful insignifi-
cancy," to which, as it seemed to him, he was
relegated, so that at the age of twenty-five, when
" many of the characters who were born for the
benefit of their fellow creatures, have rendered
themselves conspicuous among their contemporaries, . . . I still find myself as obscure, as unknown to the world, as the most indolent or the
most stupid of human beings." Entertaining
such a restless ambition, he of course accepted
the proffered office, though not without some
expression of unexplained doubt. October 31,
1794, found him at the Hague, after a voyage
of considerable peril in a leaky ship, commanded
by a blundering captain. He was a young dip-

lomat, indeed; it was on his twenty-seventh
birthday that he received his commission.

The minister made his advent upon a tu-
multuous scene. All Europe was getting under
arms in the long and desperate struggle with
France. Scarcely had he presented his credentials to the Stadtholder ere that dignitary
was obliged to flee before the conquering standards of the French. Pichegru marched into
the capital city of the Low Countries, hung
out the tri-color, and established the " Batavian
Republic" as the ally of France. The diplomatic representatives of most of the European
powers forthwith left, and Mr. Adams was
strongly moved to do the same, though for
reasons different from those which actuated
his compeers. He was not, like them, placed
in an unpleasant position by the new condition
of affairs, but on the contrary he was very cordially treated by the French and their Dutch
partisans, and was obliged to fall back upon his
native prudence to resist their compromising
overtures and dangerous friendship. Without
giving offence he yet kept clear of entanglements, and showed a degree of wisdom and
skill which many older and more experienced
Americans failed to evince, either abroad or
at home, during these exciting years. But he
appeared to be left without occupation in the

altered condition of affairs, and therefore was
considering the propriety of returning, when advices from home induced him to stay. Washington especially wrote that he must not think
of retiring, and prophesied that he would soon
be " found at the head of the diplomatic corps,
be the government administered by whomsoever
the people may choose." He remained, therefore, at the Hague, a shrewd and close observer
of the exciting events occurring around him,
industriously pursuing an extensive course of
study and reading, making useful acquaint-
ances, acquiring familiarity with foreign languages, with the usages of diplomacy and the
habits of distinguished society. He had little
public business to transact, it is true ; but at
least his time was well spent for his own improvement.

An episode in his life at the Hague was his
visit to England, where he was directed to exchange ratifications of the treaty lately negotiated by Mr. Jay. But a series of vexatious
delays, apparently maliciously contrived, de-
tained him so long that upon his arrival he
found this specific task already accomplished
by Mr. Deas. He was probably not disappointed that his name thus escaped connection
with engagements so odious to a large part of
the nation. He had, however, some further

business of an informal character to transact
with Lord Grenville, and in endeavoring to
conduct it found himself rather awkwardly
placed. He was not minister to the Court of
St. James, having been only vaguely authorized
to discuss certain arrangements in a tentative
way, without the power to enter into any definitive agreement. But the English Cabinet
strongly disliking Mr. Deas, who in the absence of Mr. Pinckney represented for the
time the United States, and much preferring
to negotiate with Mr. Adams, sought by many
indirect and artful subterfuges to thrust upon
him the character of a regularly accredited
minister. He had much ado to avoid, without
offence, the assumption of functions to which
he had no title, but which were with designing
courtesy forced upon him. His cool and moderate temper, however, carried him successfully
through the whole business, alike in its social
and its diplomatic aspect.

Another negotiation, of a private nature also,
he brought to a successful issue during these few
months in London. He made the acquaintance
of Miss Louisa Catherine Johnson, daughter
of Joshua Johnson, then American Consul at
London, and niece of that Governor Johnson, of
Maryland, who had signed the Declaration of
Independence and was afterwards placed on

the bench of the Supreme Court of the United States. To this lady he became engaged; and returning not long afterward he was married to her on July 26, 1797. It was a thoroughly happy and, for him, a life-long union.

President Washington, toward the close of his second term, transferred Mr. Adams to the Court of Portugal. But before his departure thither his destination was changed. Some degree of embarrassment was felt about this time concerning his further continuance in public office, by reason of his father's accession to the Presidency. He wrote to his mother a manly and spirited letter, rebuking her for carelessly dropping an expression indicative of a fear that he might look for some favor at his father's hands. He could neither solicit nor expect anything, he justly said, and he was pained that his mother should not know him better than to entertain any apprehension of his feeling otherwise. It was a perplexing position in which the two were placed. It would be a great hardship to cut short the son's career because of the success of the father, yet the reproach of nepotism could not be lightly encountered, even with the backing of clear consciences. Washington came kindly to the aid of his doubting successor, and in a letter highly complimentary to Mr. John Quincy Adams strongly urged that

well-merited promotion ought not to be kept
from him, foretelling for him a distinguished
future in the diplomatic service. These repre-
sentations prevailed ; and the President's only
action as concerned his son consisted in changing his destination from Portugal to Prussia,
both missions being at that time of the same
grade, though that to Prussia was then established for the first time by the making and confirming of this nomination.

To Berlin, accordingly, Mr. Adams proceeded
in November, 1797, and had the somewhat cruel
experience of being " questioned at the gates
by a dapper lieutenant, who did not know, until
one of his private soldiers explained to him, who
the United States of America were." Overcom-
ing this unusual obstacle to a ministerial advent, and succeeding, after many months, in getting through all the introductory formalities, he
found not much more to be done at Berlin than
there had been at the Hague. But such useful
work as was open to him he accomplished in the
shape of a treaty of amity and commerce between Prussia and the United States. This
having been duly ratified by both the powers,
his further stay seemed so useless that he wrote
home suggesting his readiness to return ; and
while awaiting a reply he travelled through some
portions of Europe which he had not before

seen.   His recall was one of the last.acts of his
father's administration, made, says Mr. Seward,
"that Mr. Jefferson might have no embarrassment in that direction," but quite as probably
dictated by a vindictive desire to show how wide
was the gulf of animosity which had opened between the family of the disappointed ex-President and his triumphant rival.

Mr. Adams, immediately upon his arrival at
home, prepared to return to the practice of his
profession.   It was not altogether an agreeable
transition from an embassy at the courts of Europe to a law office in Boston, with the necessity of furbishing up long disused knowledge,
and a second time patiently awaiting the influx
of clients.   But he faced it with his stubborn
temper and practical sense.   The slender promise which he was able to discern in the political
outlook could not fail to disappoint him, since
his native predilections were unquestionably and
strongly in favor of a public career.   During
his absence party animosities had been developing rapidly.   The first great party victory since
the organization of the government had just
been won, after a very bitter struggle, by the Republicans or Democrats, as they were then in-
differently called, whose exuberant delight found
its full counterpart in the angry despondency
of the Federalists.   That irascible old gentle-

man, the elder Adams, having experienced a
very Waterloo defeat in the contest for the Presidency, had ridden away from the capital, actually in a wild rage, on the night of the 3d of
March, 1801, to avoid the humiliating pageant
of Mr. Jefferson's inauguration. Yet far more
fierce than this natural party warfare was the
internal dissension which rent the Federal party
in twain. Those cracks upon the surface and
subterraneous rumblings, which the experienced
observer could for some time have noted, had
opened with terrible uproar into a gaping
chasm, when John Adams, still in the Presidency, suddenly announced his determination to
send a mission to France at a crisis when nearly
all his party were looking for war. Perhaps
this step was, as his admirers claim, an act
of pure and disinterested statesmanship. Certainly its result was fortunate for the country
at large. But for John Adams it was ruinous.
At the moment when he made the bold move,
he doubtless expected to be followed by his
party. Extreme was his disappointment and
boundless his wrath, when he found that he had
at his back only a fraction, not improbably less
than half, of that party. He learned with infinite chagrin that he had only a divided empire
with a private individual; that it was not safe
for him, the President of the United States, to

originate any important measure without first
consulting a lawyer quietly engaged in the
practice of his profession in New York; that,
in short, at least a moiety, in which were to be
found the most intelligent members, of the great
Federal party, when in search of guidance,
turned their faces toward Alexander Hamilton rather than toward John Adams. These
Hamiltonians by no means relished the French
mission, so that from this time forth a schism of
intense bitterness kept the Federal party asunder, and John Adams hated Alexander Hamilton
with a vigor not surpassed in the annals of
human antipathies. His rage was not assuaged
by the conduct of this dreaded foe in the presidential campaign; and the defeated candidate
always preferred to charge his failure to Hamilton's machinations rather than to the real will
of the people. This, however, was unfair; it
was perfectly obvious that a majority of the
nation had embraced Jeffersonian tenets, and
that Federalism was moribund.

To this condition of affairs John Quincy
Adams returned. Fortunately he had been
compelled to bear no part in the embroilments
of the past, and his sagacity must have led him,
while listening with filial sympathy to the inter-
pretations placed upon events by his incensed
parent, yet to make liberal allowance for the

distorting effects of the old gentleman's rage.
Still it was in the main only natural for him to
regard himself as a Federalist of the Adams faction.   His proclivities had always been with that
party.   In Massachusetts the educated and well-
to-do classes were almost unanimously of that
way of thinking.   The select coterie of gentlemen in the State, who in those times bore an
active and influential part in politics, were nearly
all Hamiltonians, but the adherents of President
Adams were numerically strong.   Nor was the
younger Adams himself long left without his
private grievance against Mr. Jefferson, who
promptly used the authority vested in him by a
new statute to remove Mr. Adams from the
position of commissioner in bankruptcy, to which,
at the time of his resuming business, he had been
appointed by the judge of the district court.
Long afterward Jefferson sought to escape the
odium of this apparently malicious and, for those
days, unusual action, by a very Jeffersonian
explanation, tolerably satisfactory to those persons who believed it.

On April 5, 1802, Mr. Adams was chosen by
the Federalists of Boston to represent them in
the State Senate.   The office was at that time
still sought by men of the best ability and
position, and though it was hardly a step up-
ward on the political ladder for one who had

represented the nation in foreign parts for eight
years, yet Mr. Adams was well content to accept
it. At least it reopened the door of political
life, and moreover one of his steadfast maxims
was never to refuse any function which the
people sought to impose upon him. It is worth
noting, for its bearing upon controversies soon
to be encountered in this narrative, that forty-
eight hours had not elapsed after Mr. Adams
had taken his seat before he ventured upon a
display of independence which caused much
irritation to his Federalist associates. He had
the hardihood to propose that the Federalist
majority in the legislature should permit the
Republican minority to enjoy a proportional
representation in the council. "It was the first
act of my legislative life," he wrote many years
afterward, "and it marked the principle by
which my whole public life has been governed
from that day to this. My proposal was unsuccessful, and perhaps it forfeited whatever confidence might have been otherwise bestowed
upon me as a party follower." Indeed, all his
life long Mr. Adams was never submissive to
the party whip, but voted upon every question
precisely according to his opinion of its merits,
without the slightest regard to the political
company in which for the time being he might
find himself. A compeer of his in the United

States Senate once said of him, that he regarded
every public measure which came up as he
would a proposition in Euclid, abstracted from
any party considerations. These frequent dere-
lictions of his were at first forgiven with a
magnanimity really very creditable, so long as
it lasted, especially to the Hamiltonians in the
Federal party; and so liberal was this forbearance that when in February, 1803, the legislature
had to elect a Senator to the United States
Senate, he was chosen upon the fourth ballot by
86 votes out of 171. This was the more gratifying to him and the more handsome on the part
of the anti-Adams men in the party, because the
place was eagerly sought by Timothy Pickering,
an old man who had strong claims growing out
of an almost life-long and very efficient service
in their ranks, and who was moreover a most
stanch adherent of General Hamilton.

So in October, 1803, we find Mr. Adams on
his way to Washington, the raw and unattractive village which then constituted the national
capital, wherein there was not, as the pious New
Englander instantly noted, a church of any de-
nomination ; but those who were religiously disposed were obliged to attend services " usually
performed on Sundays at the Treasury Office
and at the Capitol." With what anticipations
Mr. Adams's mind was filled during his journey

to this embryotic city his Diary does not tell;
but if they were in any degree cheerful or sanguine they were destined to cruel disappointment. He was now probably to appreciate for
the first time the fierce vigor of the hostility
which his father had excited. In Massachusetts
social connections and friendships probably mitigated the open display of rancor to which in
Washington full sway was given. It was not
only the Republican majority who showed feelings which in them were at least fair if they
were strong, but the Federal minority were maliciously pleased to find in the son of the ill-
starred John Adams a victim on whom to vent
that spleen and abuse which were so provokingly
ineffective against the solid working majority of
their opponents in Congress. The Republicans
trampled upon the Federalists, and the Federalists trampled on John Quincy Adams. He spoke
seldom and certainly did not weary the Senators, yet whenever he rose to his feet he was sure
of a cold, too often almost an insulting, reception. By no chance or possibility could anything which he said or suggested please his prejudiced auditors. The worst augury for any
measure was his support; any motion which he
made was sure to be voted down, though not
unfrequently substantially the same matter being afterward moved by somebody else would

be readily carried. That cordiality, assistance,
and sense of fellowship which Senators from the
same State customarily expect and obtain from
each other could not be enjoyed by him. For
shortly after his arrival in Washington, Mr.
Pickering had been chosen to fill a vacancy
in the other Massachusetts senatorship, and appeared upon the scene as a most unwelcome
colleague. For a time, indeed, an outward sem-
blance of political comradeship was maintained
between them, but it would have been folly for
an Adams to put faith in a Pickering, and perhaps *vice versa*. This position of his, as the
unpopular member of an unpopular minority,
could not be misunderstood, and many allusions
to it occur in his Diary. One day he notes a
motion rejected ; another day, that he has " nothing to do but to make fruitless opposition ; "
he constantly recites that he has voted with a
small minority, and at least once he himself
composed the whole of that minority ; soon after
his arrival he says that an amendment proposed
by him " will certainly not pass ; and, indeed, I
have already seen enough to ascertain that no
amendments of my proposing will obtain in the
Senate as now filled ; " again, " I presented my
three resolutions, which raised a storm as violent
as I expected ; " and on the same day he writes,
" I have no doubt of incurring much censure

and obloquy for this measure ; " a day or two
later he speaks of certain persons " who hate
me rather more than they love any principle ; "
when he expressed an opinion in favor of ratify-
ing a treaty with the Creeks, he remarks quite
philosophically, that he believes it " surprised
almost every member of the Senate, and dissatisfied almost all ; " when he wanted a committee raised he did not move it himself, but
suggested the idea to another Senator, for " I
knew that if I moved it a spirit of jealousy
would immediately be raised against doing anything." Writing once of some resolutions which
he intended to propose, he says that they are
" another feather against a whirlwind. A desperate and fearful cause in which I have embarked, but I must pursue it or feel myself
either a coward or a traitor." Another time we
find a committee, of which he was a member,
making its report when he had not even been
notified of its meeting.

It would be idle to suppose that any man could
be sufficiently callous not to feel keenly such
treatment. Mr. Adams was far from callous
and he felt it deeply. But he was not crushed
or discouraged by it, as weaker spirits would
have been, nor betrayed into any acts of foolish
anger which must have recoiled upon himself.
In him warm feelings were found in singular

combination with a cool head. An unyielding
temper and an obstinate courage, an invincible
confidence in his own judgment, and a stern
conscientiousness carried him through these earlier years of severe trial as they had afterwards
to carry him through many more. " The qualities of mind most peculiarly called for," he
reflects in the Diary, " are firmness, perseverance, patience, coolness, and forbearance. The
prospect is not promising ; yet the part to act
may be as honorably performed as if success
could attend it." He understood the situation
perfectly and met it with a better skill than that
of the veteran politician. By a long and tedious
but sure process he forced his way to steadily
increasing influence, and by the close of his
fourth year we find him taking a part in the
business of the Senate which may be fairly
called prominent and important. He was conquering success.

But if Mr. Adams's unpopularity was partly
due to the fact that he was the son of his father,
it was also largely attributable not only to his
unconciliatory manners but to more substantial
habits of mind and character. It is probably
impossible for any public man, really independent
in his political action, to lead a very comfortable life amid the struggles of party. Under
the disadvantages involved in this habit Mr.

Adams labored to a remarkable degree. Since
parties were first organized in this Republic no
American statesman has ever approached him in
persistent freedom of thought, speech, and action. He was regarded as a Federalist, but his
Federalism was subject to many modifications;
the members of that party never were sure of
his adherence, and felt bound to him by no very
strong ties of political fellowship. Towards the
close of his senatorial term he recorded, in
reminiscence, that he had more often voted with
the administration than with the opposition.

The first matter of importance concerning
which he was obliged to act was the acquisition of Louisiana and its admission as a state of
the Union. The Federalists were bitterly opposed to this measure, regarding it as an undue
strengthening of the South and of the slavery
influence, to the destruction of the fair balance
of power between the two great sections of the
country. It was not then the moral aspect of
the slavery element which stirred the northern
temper, but only the antagonism of interests
between the commercial cities of the North and
the agricultural communities of the South. In
the discussions and votes which took place in
this business Mr. Adams was in favor of the
purchase, but denied with much emphasis the
constitutionality of the process by which the

purchased territory was brought into the fellowship of States. This imperfect allegiance to the
party gave more offence than satisfaction, and
he found himself soundly berated in leading
Federalist newspapers in New England, and
angrily threatened with expulsion from the party.
But in the famous impeachment of Judge Chase,
which aroused very strong feelings, Mr. Adams
was fortunately able to vote for acquittal. He
regarded this measure, as well as the impeachment of Judge Pickering at the preceding
session, as parts of an elaborate scheme on the
part of the President for degrading the national
judiciary and rendering it subservient to the
legislative branch of the government. So many,
however, even of Mr. Jefferson's stanch adherents revolted against his requisitions on this
occasion, and he himself so far lost heart before
the final vote was taken, that several Republicans voted with the Federalists, and Mr. Adams
could hardly claim much credit with his party
for standing by them in this emergency.

It takes a long while for such a man to secure
respect, and great ability for him ever to achieve
influence. In time, however, Mr. Adams saw
gratifying indications that he was acquiring
both, and in February, 1806, we find him
writing : —

"This is the third session I have sat in Congress.

I came in as a member of a very small minority, and during the two former sessions almost uniformly avoided to take a lead; any other course would have been dishonest or ridiculous. On the very few and unimportant objects which I did undertake, I met at first with universal opposition. The last session my influence rose a little, at the present it has hitherto been apparently rising."

He was so far a cool and clear-headed judge, even in his own case, that this encouraging estimate may be accepted as correct upon his sole authority without other evidence. But the fair prospect was overcast almost in its dawning, and a period of supreme trial and of apparently irretrievable ruin was at hand.

Topics were coming forward for discussion concerning which no American could be indifferent, and no man of Mr. Adams's spirit could be silent. The policy of Great Britain towards this country, and the manner in which it was to be met, stirred profound feelings and opened such fierce dissensions as it is now difficult to appreciate. For a brief time Mr. Adams was to be a prominent actor before the people. It is fortunately needless to repeat, as it must ever be painful to remember, the familiar and too humiliating tale of the part which France and England were permitted for so many years to play in our national politics, when our par-

ties were not divided upon American questions,
but wholly by their sympathies with one or
other of these contending European powers.
Under Washington the English party had, with
infinite difficulty, been able to prevent their adversaries from fairly enlisting the United States
as active partisans of France, in spite of the
fact that most insulting treatment was received
from that country. Under John Adams the
same so-called British faction had been baulked
in their hope of precipitating a war with the
French. Now in Mr. Jefferson's second administration, the French party having won the ascendant, the new phase of the same long struggle presented the question, whether or not we
should be drawn into a war with Great Britain.
Grave as must have been the disasters of such a
war in 1806, grave as they were when the war
actually came six years later, yet it is impossible to recall the provocations which were inflicted upon us without almost regretting that
prudence was not cast to the winds and any
woes encountered in preference to unresisting
submission to such insolent outrages. Our
gorge rises at the narration three quarters of a
century after the acts were done.

Mr. Adams took his position early and boldly.
In February, 1806, he introduced into the Senate certain resolutions strongly condemnatory of

the right, claimed and vigorously exercised by
the British, of seizing neutral vessels employed
in conducting with the enemies of Great Britain any trade which had been customarily pro-
hibited by that enemy in time of peace. This
doctrine was designed to shut out American
merchants from certain privileges in trading
with French colonies, which had been accorded
only since France had become involved in war
with Great Britain. The principle was utterly
illegal and extremely injurious. Mr. Adams,
in his first resolution, stigmatized it " as an un-
provoked aggression upon the property of the
citizens of these United States, a violation of
their neutral rights, and an encroachment upon
their national independence." By his second
resolution, the President was requested to demand and insist upon the restoration of property seized under this pretext, and upon indemnification for property already confiscated. By
a rare good fortune, Mr. Adams had the pleasure of seeing his propositions carried, only
slightly modified by the omission of the words
" to insist." But they were carried, of course,
by Republican votes, and they by no means advanced their mover in the favor of the Federalist party. Strange as it may seem, that party,
of which many of the foremost supporters were
engaged in the very commerce which Great

Britain aimed to suppress and destroy, seemed not to be so much incensed against her as against their own government. The theory of the party was, substantially, that England had been driven into these measures by the friendly tone of our government towards France, and by her own stringent and overruling necessities. The cure was not to be sought in resistance, not even in indignation and remonstrance addressed to that power, but rather in cementing an alliance with her, and even, if need should be, in taking active part in her holy cause. The feeling seemed to be that we merited the chastisement because we had not allied ourselves with the chastiser. These singular notions of the Federalists, however, were by no means the notions of Mr. John Quincy Adams, as we shall soon see.

On April 18, 1806, the Non-importation Act received the approval of the President. It was the first measure indicative of resentment or retaliation which was taken by our government. When it was upon its passage it encountered the vigorous resistance of the Federalists, but received the support of Mr. Adams. On May 16, 1806, the British government made another long stride in the course of lawless oppression of neutrals, which phrase, as commerce then was, signified little else than Americans. A

proclamation was issued declaring the whole
coast of the European continent, from Brest to
the mouth of the Elbe, to be under blockade.
In fact, of course, the coast was not blockaded,
and the proclamation was a falsehood, an unjustifiable effort to make words do the work of
war-ships. The doctrine which it was thus endeavored to establish had never been admitted
into international law, has ever since been repudiated by universal consent of all nations,
and is intrinsically preposterous. The British,
however, designed to make it effective, and set
to work in earnest to confiscate all vessels and
cargoes captured on their way from any neutral
nation to any port within the proscribed district. On November 21, next following, Napoleon retaliated by the Berlin decree, so called,
declaring the entire British Isles to be under
blockade, and forbidding any vessel which had
been in any English port after publication of
his decree to enter any port in the dominions
under his control. In January, 1807, England
made the next move by an order, likewise in
contravention of international law, forbidding
to neutrals all commerce between ports of the
enemies of Great Britain. On November 11,
1807, the famous British Order in Council was
issued, declaring neutral vessels and cargoes
bound to any port or colony of any country

with which England was then at war, and
which was closed to English ships, to be liable
to capture and confiscation. A few days later,
November 25, 1807, another Order established
a rate of duties to be paid in England upon all
neutral merchandise which should be permitted
to be carried in neutral bottoms to countries
at war with that power. December 17, 1807,
Napoleon retorted by the Milan decree, which
declared denationalized and subject to capture
and condemnation every vessel, to whatsoever
nation belonging, which should have submitted
to search by an English ship, or should be on a
voyage to England, or should have paid any tax
to the English government. All these regulations, though purporting to be aimed at neutrals
generally, in fact bore almost exclusively upon
the United States, who alone were undertaking
to conduct any neutral commerce worthy of
mention. As Mr. Adams afterwards remarked,
the effect of these illegal proclamations and unjustifiable novel doctrines " placed the commerce and shipping of the United States, with
regard to all Europe and European colonies
(Sweden alone excepted), in nearly the same
state as it would have been, if, on that same
11th of November, England and France had
both declared war against the United States."
The merchants of this country might as well

have burned their ships as have submitted to
these decrees.

All this while the impressment of American
seamen by British ships of war was being vigorously prosecuted. This is one of those outrages
so long ago laid away among the mouldering
tombs in the historical graveyard that few persons now appreciate its enormity, or the extent
to which it was carried. Those who will be at
the pains to ascertain the truth in the matter
will feel that the bloodiest, most costly, and most
disastrous war would have been better than tame
endurance of treatment so brutal and unjustifiable
that it finds no parallel even in the long and dark
list of wrongs which Great Britain has been wont
to inflict upon all the weaker or the uncivilized
peoples with whom she has been brought or has
gratuitously forced herself into unwelcome contact. It was not an occasional act of high-handed
arrogance that was done; there were not only a
few unfortunate victims, of whom a large proportion might be of unascertained nationality.
It was an organized system worked upon a very
large scale. Every American seaman felt it
necessary to have a certificate of citizenship,
accompanied by a description of his features and
of all the marks upon his person, as Mr. Adams
said, "like the advertisement for a runaway negro
slave." Nor was even this protection by any

means sure to be always efficient. The number
of undoubted American citizens who were seized
rose in a few years actually to many thousands.
They were often taken without so much as a
false pretence to right; but with the acknow-
ledgment that they were Americans, they were
seized upon the plea of a necessity for their
services in the British ship. Some American
vessels were left so denuded of seamen that they
were lost at sea for want of hands to man them;
the destruction of lives as well as property, unquestionably thus caused, was immense. When
after the lapse of a long time and of infinite
negotiation the American citizenship of some
individual was clearly shown, still the chances of
his return were small; some false and ignoble
subterfuge was resorted to; he was not to be
found; the name did not occur on the rolls of
the navy; he had died, or been discharged, or
had deserted, or had been shot. The more
illegal the act committed by any British officer
the more sure he was of reward, till it seemed
that the impressment of American citizens was
an even surer road to promotion than valor in
an engagement with the enemy. Such were the
substantial wrongs inflicted by Great Britain;
nor were any pains taken to cloak their character;
on the contrary, they were done with more than
British insolence and offensiveness, and were

accompanied with insults which alone constituted
sufficient provocation to war. To all this, for a
long time, nothing but empty and utterly futile
protests were opposed by this country. The affair
of the Chesapeake, indeed, threatened for a brief
moment to bring things to a crisis. That vessel, an American frigate, commanded by Com-
modore Barron, sailed on June 22, 1807, from
Hampton Roads. The Leopard, a British fifty-
gun ship, followed her, and before she was out
of sight of land, hailed her and demanded the
delivery of four men, of whom three at least
were surely native Americans. Barron refused
the demand, though his ship was wholly unpre-
pared for action. Thereupon the Englishman
opened his broadsides, killed three men and
wounded sixteen, boarded the Chesapeake and
took off the four sailors. They were carried to
Halifax and tried by court-martial for desertion :
one of them was hanged ; one died in confine-
ment, and five years elapsed before the other
two were returned to the Chesapeake in Boston
harbor. This wound was sufficiently deep to
arouse a real spirit of resentment and revenge,
and England went so far as to dispatch Mr.
Rose to this country upon a pretended mission
of peace, though the fraudulent character of his
errand was sufficiently indicated by the fact
that within a few hours after his departure the

first of the above named Orders in Council was
issued but had not been communicated to him.
As Mr. Adams indignantly said, "the same pen-
ful of ink which signed his instructions might
have been used also to sign these illegal orders."
Admiral Berkeley, the commander of the Leopard, received the punishment which he might
justly have expected if precedent was to count
for anything in the naval service of Great
Britain, — he was promoted.

It is hardly worth while to endeavor to measure
the comparative wrongfulness of the conduct of
England and of France. The behavior of each
was utterly unjustifiable; though England by
committing the first extreme breach of international law gave to France the excuse of retaliation.
There was, however, vast difference in the
practical effect of the British and French decrees.
The former wrought serious injury, falling little
short of total destruction, to American shipping
and commerce; the latter were only in a much
less degree hurtful. The immense naval power
of England and the channels in which our trade
naturally flowed combined to make her destruc-
tive capacity as towards us very great. It was
the outrages inflicted by her which brought the
merchants of the United States face to face with
ruin; they suffered not very greatly at the hands
of Napoleon. Neither could the villainous process

of impressment be conducted by Frenchmen.
France gave us cause for war, but England
seemed resolved to drive us into it.

As British aggressions grew steadily and rapidly more intolerable, Mr. Adams found himself
straining farther and farther away from those
Federalist moorings at which, it must be confessed, he had long swung very precariously.
The constituency which he represented was indeed in a quandary so embarrassing as hardly to
be capable of maintaining any consistent policy.
The New England of that day was a trading
community, of which the industry and capital
were almost exclusively centred in ship-owning
and commerce. The merchants, almost to a
man, had long been the most Anglican of Federalists in their political sympathies. Now they
found themselves suffering utterly ruinous treatment at the hands of those whom they had
loved overmuch. They were being ruthlessly
destroyed by their friends, to whom they had
been, so to speak, almost disloyally loyal. They
saw their business annihilated, their property
seized, and yet could not give utterance to resentment, or counsel resistance, without such a
humiliating devouring of all their own principles and sentiments as they could by no possibility bring themselves to endure. There was
but one road open to them, and that was the

ignoble one of casting themselves wholly into
the arms of England, of rewarding her blows
with caresses, of submitting to be fairly scourged
into a servile alliance with her. It is not surprising that the independent temper of Mr.
Adams revolted at the position which his party
seemed not reluctant to assume at this juncture.
Yet not very much better seemed for a time
the policy of the administration. Jefferson was
far from being a man for troubled seasons,
which called for high spirit and executive energy. His flotillas of gunboats and like idle
and silly fantasies only excited Mr. Adams's
disgust. In fact, there was upon all sides a
strong dread of a war with England, not always
openly expressed, but now perfectly visible, arising with some from regard for that country, in
others prompted by fear of her power. Alone
among public men Mr. Adams, while earnestly
hoping to escape war, was not willing to seek
that escape by unlimited weakness and unbounded submission to lawless injury.

On November 17, 1807, Mr. Adams, who
never in his life allowed fear to become a motive, wrote, with obvious contempt and indignation : " I observe among the members great
embarrassment, alarm, anxiety, and confusion
of mind, but no preparation for any measure
of vigor, and an obvious strong disposition to

yield all that Great Britain may require, to preserve peace, under a thin external show of dignity and bravery." This tame and vacillating
spirit roused his ire, and as it was chiefly manifested by his own party it alienated him from
them farther than ever. Yet his wrath was so
far held in reasonable check by his discretion
that he would still have liked to avoid the perilous conclusion of arms, and though his impulse
was to fight, yet he could not but recognize that
the sensible course was to be content, for the
time at least, with a manifestation of resentment, and the most vigorous acts short of war
which the government could be induced to undertake. On this sentiment were based his in-
troduction of the aforementioned resolutions, his
willingness to support the administration, and
his vote for the Non-importation Act in spite of
a dislike for it as a very imperfectly satisfactory
measure. But it was not alone his naturally independent temper which led him thus to feel so
differently from other members of his party. In
Europe he had had opportunities of forming a
judgment more accurate than was possible for
most Americans concerning the sentiments and
policy of England towards this country. Not
only had he been present at the negotiations
resulting in the treaty of peace, but he had also
afterwards been for several months engaged in

the personal discussion of commercial questions
with the British minister of foreign affairs.
From all that he had thus seen and heard he
had reached the conviction, unquestionably correct, that the British were not only resolved to
adopt a selfish course towards the United States,
which might have been expected, but that they
were consistently pursuing the further distinct
design of crippling and destroying American
commerce, to the utmost degree which their own
extensive trade and great naval authority and
power rendered possible. So long as he held
this firm belief, it was inevitable that he should
be at issue with the Federalists in all matters
concerning our policy towards Great Britain.
The ill-will naturally engendered in him by
this conviction was increased to profound indignation when illiberal measures were succeeded by insults, by substantial wrongs in direct contravention of law, and by acts properly
to be described as of real hostility. For Mr.
Adams was by nature not only independent, but
resentful and combative. When, soon after the
attack of the Leopard upon the Chesapeake, he
heard the transaction "openly justified at noon-
day," by a prominent Federalist,[1] "in a public
insurance office upon the exchange at Boston,"
his temper rose. "This," he afterward wrote,

---

[1] Mr. John Lowell.

"this was the cause . . . which alienated me
from that day and forever from the councils of
the Federal party." When the news of that
outrage reached Boston, Mr. Adams was there,
and desired that the leading Federalists in
the city should at once "take the lead in promoting a strong and clear expression of the
sentiments of the people, and in an open and
free-hearted manner, setting aside all party feelings, declare their determination at that crisis
to support the government of their country."
But unfortunately these gentlemen were by no
means prepared for any such action, and fool-
ishly left it for the friends of the administration
to give the first utterance to a feeling which it
is hard to excuse any American for not entertaining beneath such provocation. It was the
Jeffersonians, accordingly, who convened "an
informal meeting of the citizens of Boston and
the neighboring towns," at which Mr. Adams
was present, and by which he was put upon
a committee to draw and report resolutions.
These resolutions pledged a cheerful coöpera-
tion "in any measures, however serious," which
the government might deem necessary and a
support of the same with "lives and fortunes."
The Federalists, learning too late that their
backwardness at this crisis was a blunder,
caused a town meeting to be called at Faneuil

Hall a few days later. This also Mr. Adams attended, and again was put on the committee to draft resolutions, which were only a little less strong than those of the earlier assemblage. But though many of the Federalists thus tardily and reluctantly fell in with the popular sentiment, they were for the most part heartily incensed against Mr. Adams. They threatened him that he should " have his head taken off for apostasy," and gave him to understand that he " should no longer be considered as having any communion with the party." If he had not already quite left them, they now turned him out from their community. But such abusive treatment was ill adapted to influence a man of his temper. Martyrdom, which in time he came to relish, had not now any terrors for him ; and he would have lost as many heads as ever grew on Hydra, ere he would have yielded on a point of principle.

His spirit was soon to be demonstrated. Congress was convened in extra session on October 26, 1807. The administration brought forward the bill establishing an embargo. The measure may now be pronounced a blunder, and its proposal created a howl of rage and anguish from the commercial states, who saw in it only their utter ruin. Already a strong sectional feeling had been developed between

the planters of the South and the merchants of
the North and East, and the latter now united
in the cry that their quarter was to be ruined
by the ignorant policy of this Virginian President. Terrible then was their wrath, when they
actually saw a Massachusetts Senator boldly give
his vote for what they deemed the most odious
and wicked bill which had ever been presented
in the halls of Congress. Nay, more, they
learned with horror that Mr. Adams had even
been a member of the committee which reported
the bill, and that he had joined in the report.
Henceforth the Federal party was to be like a
hive of enraged hornets about the devoted ren-
egade. No abuse which they could heap upon
him seemed nearly adequate to the occasion.
They despised him ; they loathed him ; they said
and believed that he was false, selfish, designing,
a traitor, an apostate, that he had run away
from a failing cause, that he had sold himself.
The language of contumely was exhausted in
vain efforts to describe his baseness. Not even
yet has the echo of the hard names which he
was called quite died away in the land ; and
there are still families in New England with
whom his dishonest tergiversation remains a
traditional belief.

Never was any man more unjustly aspersed.
It is impossible to view all the evidence dis-

passionately without not only acquitting Mr.
Adams but greatly admiring his courage, his
constancy, his independence. Whether the embargo was a wise and efficient or a futile and
useless measure has little to do with the question of his conduct. The emergency called for
strong action. The Federalists suggested only a
temporizing submission, or that we should avert
the terrible wrath of England by crawling beneath her lashes into political and commercial
servitude. Mr. Jefferson thought the embargo
would do, that it would aid him in his negotiations with England sufficiently to enable him to
bring her to terms; he had before thought the
same of the Non-importation Act. Mr. Adams
felt, properly enough, concerning both these
schemes, that they were insufficient and in
many respects objectionable; but that to give
the administration hearty support in the most
vigorous measures which it was willing to undertake, was better than to aid an opposition
utterly nerveless and servile and altogether
devoid of so much as the desire for efficient
action. It was no time to stay with the party
of weakness; it was right to strengthen rather
than to hamper a man so pacific and spiritless as
Mr. Jefferson; to show a readiness to forward
even his imperfect expedients; to display a
united and indignant, if not quite a hostile

front to Great Britain, rather than to exhibit a
tame and friendly feeling towards her. It was
for these reasons, which had already controlled
his action concerning the non-importation bill,
that Mr. Adams joined in reporting the embargo bill and voted for it. He never pretended that he himself had any especial fancy
for either of these measures, or that he regarded
them as the best that could be devised under
the circumstances. On the contrary, he hoped
that the passage of the embargo would allow of
the repeal of its predecessor. That he expected
some good from it, and that it did some little
good, cannot be denied. It did save a great deal
of American property, both shipping and merchandise, from seizure and condemnation ; and
if it cut off the income it at least saved much
of the principal of our merchants. If only the
bill had been promptly repealed so soon as this
protective purpose had been achieved, without
awaiting further and altogether impossible ben-
efits to accrue from it as an offensive measure,
it might perhaps have left a better memory behind it. Unfortunately no one can deny that it
was continued much too long. Mr. Adams saw
this error and dreaded the consequences. After
he had left Congress and had gone back to private life, he exerted all the influence which he
had with the Republican members of Congress

to secure its repeal and the substitution of the
Non-intercourse Act, an exchange which was in
time accomplished, though much too tardily.
Nay, much more than this, Mr. Adams stands
forth almost alone as the advocate of threatening if not of actually belligerent measures. He
expressed his belief that " our internal resources [were] competent to the establishment
and maintenance of a naval force, public and
private, if not fully adequate to the protection
and defence of our commerce, at least sufficient
to induce a retreat from hostilities, and to deter
from a renewal of them by either of the war-
ring parties ; " and he insisted that " a system to
that effect might be formed, ultimately far more
economical, and certainly more energetic," than
the embargo. But his " resolution met no encouragement." He found that it was the embargo or nothing, and he thought the embargo
was a little better than nothing, as probably it
was.

All the arguments which Mr. Adams advanced were far from satisfying his constituents
in those days of wild political excitement, and
they quickly found the means of intimating their
unappeasable displeasure in a way certainly not
open to misapprehension. Mr. Adams's term
of service in the Senate was to expire on March
3, 1809. On June 2 and 3, 1808, anticipating by

many months the customary time for filling the
coming vacancy, the legislature of Massachusetts
proceeded to choose James Lloyd, junior, his
successor. The votes were, in the Senate 21 for
Mr. Lloyd, 17 for Mr. Adams; in the House
248 for Mr. Lloyd, and 213 for Mr. Adams. A
more insulting method of administering a re-
buke could not have been devised. At the same
time, in further expression of disapprobation,
resolutions strongly condemnatory of the embargo were passed. Mr. Adams was not the
man to stay where he was not wanted, and on
June 8 he sent in his letter of resignation. On
the next day Mr. Lloyd was chosen to serve for
the balance of his term.

Thus John Quincy Adams changed sides.
The son of John Adams lost the senatorship
for persistently supporting the administration
of Thomas Jefferson. It was indeed a singular
spectacle! In 1803 he had been sent to the
Senate of the United States by Federalists as
a Federalist; in 1808 he had abjured them and
they had repudiated him; in 1809, as we are
soon to see, he received a foreign appointment
from the Republican President Madison, and
was confirmed by a Republican Senate. Many
of Mr. Adams's acts, many of his traits, have
been harshly criticised, but for no act that he
ever did or ever was charged with doing has

he been so harshly assailed as for this journey
from one camp to the other. The gentlemen
of wealth, position, and influence in Eastern
Massachusetts, almost to a man, turned against
him with virulence; many of their descendants
still cherish the ancestral prejudice; and it may
yet be a long while before the last mutterings
of this deep-rooted antipathy die away. But
that they will die away in time cannot be
doubted. Praise will succeed to blame. Truth
must prevail in a case where such abundant
evidence is accessible; and the truth is that Mr.
Adams's conduct was not ignoble, mean, and
traitorous, but honorable, courageous, and disinterested. Those who singled him out for
assault, though deaf to his arguments, might
even then have reflected that within a few years
a large proportion of the whole nation had
changed in their opinions as he had now at last
changed in his, so that the party which under
Washington hardly had an existence and under
John Adams was not, until the last moment,
seriously feared, now showed an enormous majority throughout the whole country. Even in
Massachusetts, the intrenched camp of the Federalists, one half of the population were now
Republicans. But that change of political sentiment which in the individual voter is often
admired as evidence of independent thought is

stigmatized in those more prominent in politics as tergiversation and apostasy.

It may be admitted that there are sound reasons for holding party leaders to a more rigid allegiance to party policy than is expected of the rank and file ; yet certainly, at those periods when substantially new measures and new doctrines come to the front, the old party names lose whatever sacredness may at other times be in them, and the political fellowships of the past may properly be reformed. Novel problems cannot always find old comrades still united in opinions. Precisely such was the case with John Quincy Adams and the Federalists. The earlier Federalist creed related to one set of issues, the later Federalist creed to quite another set ; the earlier creed was sound and deserving of support ; the later creed was not so. It is easy to see, as one looks backward upon history, that every great and successful party has its mission, that it wins its success through the substantial righteousness of that mission, and that it owes its downfall to assuming an erroneous attitude towards some subsequent matter which becomes in turn of predominating importance. Sometimes, though rarely, a party remains on the right side through two or even more successive issues of profound consequence to the nation. The Federalist mis-

sion was to establish the Constitution of the
United States as a vigorous, efficient, and practical system of government, to prove its sound-
ness, safety, and efficacy, and to defend it from
the undermining assaults of those who dis-
trusted it and would have reduced it to imbecility. Supplementary and cognate to this was
the further task of giving the young nation and
the new system a chance to get fairly started in
life before being subjected to the strain of war
and European entanglements. To this end it
was necessary to hold in check the Jeffersonian
or French party, who sought to embroil us in
a foreign quarrel. These two functions of the
Federalist party were quite in accord; they involved the organizing and domestic instinct
against the disorganizing and meddlesome; the
strengthening against the enfeebling process;
practical thinking against fanciful theories. Fortunately the able men had been generally of the
sound persuasion, and by powerful exertions had
carried the day and accomplished their allotted
tasks so thoroughly that all subsequent generations of Americans have been reaping the benefit of their labors. But by the time that John
Adams had concluded his administration the
great Federalist work had been sufficiently done.
Those who still believe that there is an overruling Providence in the affairs of men and na-

tions may well point to the history of this
period in support of their theory. Republican-
ism was not able to triumph till Federalism had
fulfilled all its proper duty and was on the point
of going wrong.

During this earlier period John Quincy Adams
had been a Federalist by conviction as well as
by education. Nor was there any obvious reason
for him to change his political faith with the
change of party success, brought about as that
was before its necessity was apparent but by
the sure and inscrutable wisdom so marvellously
enclosed in the great popular instinct. It was
not patent, when Mr. Jefferson succeeded Mr.
Adams, that Federalism was soon to become
an unsound political creed — unsound, not because it had been defeated, but because it had
done its work, and in the new emergency was
destined to blunder. During Mr. Jefferson's
first administration no questions of novel import arose. But they were not far distant, and
soon were presented by the British aggressions.
A grave crisis was created by this system of
organized destruction of property and wholesale
stealing of citizens, now suddenly practised with
such terrible energy. What was to be done ?
What had the two great parties to advise concerning the policy of the country in this hour of
peril ? Unfortunately for the Federalists old

predilections were allowed now to govern their
present action. Excusably Anglican in the bygone days of Genet's mission, they now remained still Anglican, when to be Anglican was
to be emphatically un-American. As one reads
the history of 1807 and 1808 it is impossible
not to feel almost a sense of personal gratitude
to John Quincy Adams that he dared to step
out from his meek-spirited party and do all that
circumstances rendered possible to promote resistance to insults and wrongs intolerable. In
truth, he was always a man of high temper, and
eminently a patriotic citizen of the United
States. Unlike too many even of the best
among his countrymen in those early years of
the Republic, he had no foreign sympathies
whatsoever; he was neither French nor English,
but wholly, exclusively, and warmly American.
He had no second love; the United States
filled his public heart and monopolized his political affections. When he was abroad he established neither affiliations nor antipathies,
and when he was at home he drifted with no
party whose course was governed by foreign
magnets. It needs only that this characteristic
should be fully understood in order that his
conduct in 1808 should be not alone vindicated
but greatly admired.

At that time it was said, and it has been since

repeated, that he was allured by the loaves and
fishes which the Republicans could distribute,
while the Federalists could cast to him only
meagre and uncertain crusts. Circumstances
gave to the accusation such a superficial plau-
sibility that it was believed by many honest
men under the influence of political prejudice.
But such a charge, alleged concerning a single
act in a long public career, is to be scanned
with suspicion. Disproof by demonstration is
impossible ; but it is fair to seek for the character of the act in a study of the character of the
actor, as illustrated by the rest of his career.
Thus seeking we shall see that, if any traits can
be surely predicated of any man, independence,
courage, and honesty may be predicated of Mr.
Adams. His long public life had many periods
of trial, yet this is the sole occasion when it is
so much as possible seriously to question the
purity of his motives — for the story of his intrigue with Mr. Clay to secure the Presidency
was never really believed by any one except
General Jackson, and the beliefs of General
Jackson are of little consequence. From the
earliest to the latest day of his public life, he
was never a party man. He is entitled to the
justification to be derived from this life-long
habit, when, in 1807-8, he voted against the
wishes of those who had hoped to hold him in

the bonds of partisan alliance. In point of fact,
so far from these acts being a yielding to selfish
and calculating temptation, they called for great
courage and strength of mind ; instead of being
tergiversation, they were a triumph in a severe
ordeal. Mr. Adams was not so dull as to under-
rate, nor so void of good feeling as to be careless of, the storm of obloquy which he had to
encounter, not only in such shape as is customary in like instances of a change of sides in
politics, but, in his present case, of a peculiarly
painful kind. He was to seem unfaithful, not
only to a party, but to the bitter feud of a father whom he dearly loved and greatly respected ; he was to be reviled by the neighbors
and friends who constituted his natural social
circle in Boston ; he was to alienate himself
from the rich, the cultivated, the influential
gentlemen of his neighborhood, his comrades,
who would almost universally condemn his conduct. He was to lose his position as Senator,
and probably to destroy all hopes of further
political success so far as it depended upon the
good will of the people of his own State. In
this he was at least giving up a certainty in exchange for what even his enemies must admit to
have been only an expectation.

But in fact it is now evident that there was
not upon his part even an expectation. At the

first signs of the views which he was likely to
hold, that contemptible but influential Republican, Giles, of Virginia, also one or two others
of the same party, sought to approach him with
insinuating suggestions.   But Mr. Adams met
these advances in a manner frigid and repellent
even beyond his wont, and far from seeking to
conciliate these emissaries, and to make a bargain, or even establish a tacit understanding for
his own benefit, he held them far aloof, and simply stated that he wished and expected nothing
from the administration.   His mind was made
up, his opinion was formed; no bribe was needed
to secure his vote.   Not thus do men sell themselves in politics.   The Republicans were fairly
notified that he was going to do just as he
chose; and Mr. Jefferson, the arch-enemy of all
Adamses, had no occasion to forego his feud to
win this recruit from that family.

Mr. Adams's Diary shows unmistakably that
he was acting rigidly upon principle, that he
believed himself to be injuring or even destroying his political prospects, and that in so doing he taxed his moral courage severely.   The
whole tone of the Diary, apart from those few
distinct statements which hostile critics might
view with distrust, is despondent, often bitter,
but defiant and stubborn.   If in later life he
ever anticipated the possible publication of these

private pages, yet he could hardly have done
so at this early day. Among certain general
reflections at the close of the year 1808, he
writes: "On most of the great national questions now under discussion, my sense of duty
leads me to support the Administration, and I
find myself, of course, in opposition to the Federalists in general. But I have no communication with the President, other than that in the
regular order of business in the Senate. In this
state of things my situation calls in a peculiar
manner for prudence; my political prospects
are declining, and, as my term of service draws
near its close, I am constantly approaching to
the certainty of being restored to the situation
of a private citizen. For this event, however,
I hope to have my mind sufficiently prepared."

In July, 1808, the Republicans of the Congressional District wished to send him to the
House of Representatives, but to the gentleman who waited upon him with this proposal
he returned a decided negative. Other considerations apart, he would not interfere with the
reëlection of his friend, Mr. Quincy.

Certain remarks, written when his senatorial
term was far advanced, when he had lost the
confidence of the Federalists without obtaining
that of the Republicans, may be of interest at
this point. He wrote, October 30, 1807: "I

employed the whole evening in looking over
the Journal of the Senate, since I have been
one of its members. Of the very little business
which I have commenced during the four sessions, at least three fourths has failed, with circumstances of peculiar mortification. The very
few instances in which I have succeeded, have
been always after an opposition of great obstinacy, often ludicrously contrasting with the in-
significance of the object in pursuit. More
than one instance has occurred where the same
thing which I have assiduously labored in vain
to effect has been afterwards accomplished by
others, without the least resistance; more than
once, where the pleasure of disappointing me
has seemed to be the prominent principle of
decision. Of the preparatory business, matured
in committees, I have had a share, gradually increasing through the four sessions, but always
as a subordinate member. The merely laborious duties have been readily assigned to me, and
as readily undertaken and discharged. My success has been more frequent in opposition than
in carrying any proposition of my own, and I
hope I have been instrumental in arresting many
unadvised purposes and projects. Though as
to the general policy of the country I have
been uniformly in a small, and constantly de-
ceasing minority; my opinions and votes have

been much oftener in unison with the Administration than with their opponents; I have met with at least as much opposition from my party friends as from their adversaries, — I believe more. I know not that I have made any personal enemies now in Senate, nor can I flatter myself with having acquired any personal friends. There have been hitherto two, Mr. Tracey and Mr. Plumer, upon whom I could rely, but it has pleased Providence to remove one by death, and the changes of political party have removed the other." This is a striking paragraph, certainly not written by a man in a very cheerful or sanguine frame of mind, not by one who congratulates himself on having skilfully taken the initial steps in a brilliant political career; but, it is fair to say, by one who has at least tried to do his duty, and who has not knowingly permitted himself to be warped either by passion, prejudice, party alliances, or selfish considerations.

As early as November, 1805, Mr. Adams, being still what may be described as an independent Federalist, was approached by Dr. Rush with tentative suggestions concerning a foreign mission. Mr. Madison, then Secretary of State, and even President Jefferson were apparently not disinclined to give him such employment, provided he would be willing to accept it at their hands. Mr. Adams simply replied, that he would not refuse a nomination merely because it came from Mr. Jefferson, though there was no office in the President's gift for which he had any wish. Perhaps because of the unconciliatory coolness of this response, or perhaps for some better reason, the nomination did not follow at that time. No sooner, however, had Mr. Madison fairly taken the oath of office as President than he bethought him of Mr. Adams, now no longer a Federalist, but, concerning the present issues, of the Republican persuasion. On March 6, 1809, Mr. Adams was notified by the President personally of the intention to nominate him as Minister Plenipotentiary to Russia. It was a new mission, the first minister ever nominated to Russia having been only a short time before rejected by the Senate. But the Emperor had often expressed his wish to exchange ministers, and Mr. Madison was anxious to comply with the courteous request. Mr. Adams's name was accordingly at once sent to the Senate. But on the following day, March 7, that body resolved that "it is inexpedient at this time to appoint a minister from the United States to the Court of Russia." The vote was seventeen to fifteen, and among the seventeen was Mr. Adams's old colleague, Timothy Pickering, who probably never in his life cast a vote which gave him so much pleasure. Mr. Madison, however, did not readily desist from his purpose, and a few months later, June 26, he sent a message to the Senate, stating that the considerations previously leading him to nominate a minister to Russia had since been strengthened, and again naming Mr. Adams for the post. This time the nomination was confirmed with readiness, by a vote of nineteen to seven, Mr. Pickering, of course, being one of the still hostile minority.

At noon on August 5, 1809, records Mr. Adams, " I left my house at the corner of Boylston and Nassau streets, in Boston," again to make the tedious and uncomfortable voyage across the Atlantic. A miserable and a dangerous time he had of it ere, on October 23, he reached St. Petersburg. Concerning the four years and a half which he is now to spend in Russia very little need be said. His active duties were of the simplest character, amounting to little more than rendering occasional assistance to American shipmasters suffering beneath the severities so often illegally inflicted by the contesting powers of Europe. But apart from the slender practical service to be done, the period must have been interesting and agreeable for him personally, for he was received and treated throughout his stay by the Emperor

and his courtiers with distinguished kindness.
The Emperor, who often met him walking,
used to stop and chat with him, while Count
Romanzoff, the minister of foreign affairs, was
cordial beyond the ordinary civility of diplomacy.   The Diary records a series of court presentations, balls, fêtes, dinners, diplomatic and
other, launches, displays of fireworks, birthday
festivities, parades, baptisms, plays, state fu-
nerals, illuminations, and Te Deums for victories ; in short, every species of social gayety and
public pageant.   At all these Mr. Adams was
always a bidden and apparently a welcome
guest.   It must be admitted, even by his de-
tractors, that he was an admirable representative of the United States abroad.   Having
already seen much of the distinguished society
of European courts, but retaining a republican
simplicity, which was wholly genuine and a
natural part of his character and therefore was
never affected or offensive in its manifestations, he really represented the best element in
the politics and society of the United States.
Winning respect for himself he won it also for
the country which he represented.   Thus he
was able to render an indirect but essential
service in cementing the kindly feeling which
the Russian Empire entertained for the American Republic.   Russia could then do us little

good and almost no harm, yet the friendship of
a great European power had a certain moral
value in those days of our national infancy.
That friendship, so cordially offered, Mr. Adams was fortunately well fitted to conciliate,
showing in his foreign callings a tact which did
not mark him in other public relations. He
was perhaps less liked by his travelling fellow
countrymen than by the Russians. The paltry
ambition of a certain class of Americans for in-
troduction to high society disgusted him greatly,
and he was not found an efficient ally by these
would-be comrades of the Russian aristocracy.
" The ambition of young Americans to crowd
themselves upon European courts and into the
company of nobility is a very ridiculous and
not a very proud feature of their character," he
wrote ; " there is nothing, in my estimate of
things, meaner than courting society where, if
admitted, it is only to be despised." He himself happily combined extensive acquirements,
excellent ability, diplomatic and courtly experience, and natural independence of character
without ill-bred self-assertion, and never failed
to create a good impression in the many circles
into which his foreign career introduced him.

The ambassadors and ministers from European powers at St. Petersburg were constantly
wrangling about precedence and like petty mat-

ters of court etiquette. " In all these controversies," writes Mr. Adams, " I have endeavored
to consider it as an affair in which I, as an
American minister, had no concern ; and that
my only principle is to dispute upon precedence
with nobody." A good-natured contempt for
European follies may be read between the lines
of this remark ; wherein it may be said that the
Monroe Doctrine is applied to court etiquette.

He always made it a point to live within the
meagre income which the United States allowed
him, but seems to have suffered no diminution
of consideration for this reason. One morning,
walking on the Fontanka, he met the Emperor,
who said : " Mons. Adams, il y a cent ans que
je ne vous ai vu ; " and then continuing the conversation, " asked me whether I intended to
take a house in the country this summer. I
said, No. . . . ' And why so ? ' said he. I was
hesitating upon an answer when he relieved me
from embarrassment by saying, ' Peutêtre sont-ce
des considerations de finance ? ' As he said it
with perfect good humor and with a smile, I
replied in the same manner : ' Mais Sire, elles
y sont pour une bonne part.' " [1]

The volume of the journal which records this
residence in St. Petersburg is very interesting
as a picture of Russian life and manners in

[1] An interesting sketch of his household and its expenses is
to be found in ii. Diary, 193.

high society. Few travellers write anything
nearly so vivid, so thorough, or so trustworthy
as these entries. Moreover, during the whole
period of his stay the great wars of Napoleon
were constantly increasing the astonishment of
mankind, and created intense excitement at the
Court of Russia. These feelings waxed stronger
as it grew daily more likely that the Emperor
would have to take his turn also as a party de-
fendant in the great conflict. Then at last
came the fact of war, the invasion of Russia,
the burning of Moscow, the disastrous retreat
of the invaders ending in ignominious flight,
the advance of the allies, finally the capture of
Paris. All this while Mr. Adams at St. Petersburg witnessed first the alarm and then the exultation of the court and the people as the
rumors now of defeat, anon of victory, were
brought by the couriers at tantalizing intervals ;
and he saw the rejoicings and illuminations
which rendered the Russian capital so brilliant
and glorious during the last portion of his residence. It was an experience well worth having,
and which is pleasantly depicted in the Diary.

In September, 1812, Count Romanzoff suggested to Mr. Adams the readiness of the Emperor to act as mediator in bringing about peace
between the United States and England. The
suggestion was promptly acted upon, but with

no directly fortunate results. The American government acceded at once to the proposition, and at the risk of an impolitic display of readiness dispatched Messrs. Gallatin and Bayard to act as Commissioners jointly with Mr. Adams in the negotiations. These gentlemen, however, arrived in St. Petersburg only to find themselves in a very awkward position. Their official character might not properly be considered as attaching unless England should accept the offer of mediation. But England had refused, in the first instance, to do this, and she now again reiterated her refusal without regard for the manifestation of willingness on the part of the United States. Further, Mr. Gallatin's nomination was rejected by the Senate after his departure, on the ground that his retention of the post of Secretary of the Treasury was incompatible, under the Constitution, with this diplomatic function. So the United States appeared in a very annoying attitude, her Commissioners were uncomfortable and somewhat humiliated; Russia felt a certain measure of vexation at the brusque and positive rejection of her friendly proposition on the part of Great Britain; and that country alone came out of the affair with any self-satisfaction.

But by the time when all hopes of peace through the friendly offices of Russia were at

an end, that stage of the conflict had been
reached at which both parties were quite ready
to desist. The United States, though triumph-
ing in some brilliant naval victories, had been
having a sorry experience on land, where, as
the Russian minister remarked, "England did
as she pleased." A large portion of the people
were extremely dissatisfied, and it was impossible to ignore that the outlook did not promise
better fortunes in the future than had been encountered in the past. On the other hand,
England had nothing substantial to expect from
a continuance of the struggle, except heavy additional expenditure which it was not then the
fashion to compel the worsted party to recoup.
She accordingly intimated her readiness to send
Commissioners to Göttingen, for which place
Ghent was afterwards substituted, to meet
American Commissioners and settle terms of
pacification. The United States renewed the
powers of Messrs. Adams, Bayard, and Gallatin, a new Secretary of the Treasury having in
the meantime been appointed, and added Jonathan Russell, then Minister to Sweden, and
Henry Clay. England deputed Lord Gambier,
an admiral, Dr. Adams, a publicist, and Mr.
Goulburn, a member of Parliament and Under
Secretary of State. These eight gentlemen accordingly met in Ghent on August 7, 1814.

It was upwards of four months before an agreement was reached. During this period Mr. Adams kept his Diary with much more even than his wonted faithfulness, and it undoubtedly presents the most vivid picture in existence of the labors of treaty-making diplomatists. The eight were certainly an odd assemblage of peace-makers. The ill-blood and wranglings between the opposing Commissions were bad enough, yet hardly equalled the intestine dissensions between the American Commissioners themselves. That the spirit of peace should ever have emanated from such an universal embroilment is almost sufficiently surprising to be regarded as a mir-acle. At the very beginning, or even before fairly beginning, the British party roused the jealous ire of the Americans by proposing that they all should meet, for exchanging their full powers, at the lodgings of the Englishmen. The Americans took fire at this "offensive pretension to superiority" which was "the usage from Ambassadors to Ministers of an inferior order." Mr. Adams cited Martens, and Mr. Bayard read a case from Ward's "Law of Nations." Mr. Adams suggested sending a pointed reply, agree-ing to meet the British Commissioners "at any place other than their own lodgings;" but Mr. Gallatin, whose valuable function was destined to be the keeping of the peace among his fractious colleagues, as well as betwixt them and the Englishmen, substituted the milder phrase, " at any place which may be mutually agreed upon." The first meeting accordingly took place at the Hôtel des Pays Bas, where it was arranged that the subsequent conferences should be held alternately at the quarters of the two Commissions. Then followed expressions, conventional and proper but wholly untrue, of mutual sentiments of esteem and good will.

No sooner did the gentlemen begin to get seriously at the work before them than the most discouraging prospects were developed. The British first presented their demands, as follows : 1. That the United States should conclude a peace with the Indian allies of Great Britain, and that a species of neutral belt of Indian territory should be established between the dominions of the United States and Great Britain, so that these dominions should be nowhere conterminous, upon which belt or barrier neither power should be permitted to encroach even by purchase, and the boundaries of which should be settled in this treaty. 2. That the United States should keep no naval force upon the Great Lakes, and should neither maintain their existing forts nor build new ones upon their northern frontier ; it was even required that the boundary line should run along the southern shore of the lakes; while no corresponding restriction was imposed upon Great Britain, because she was stated to have no projects of conquest as against her neighbor. 3. That a piece of the province of Maine should be ceded, in order to give the English a road from Halifax to Quebec. 4. That the stipulation of the treaty of 1783, conferring on English subjects the right of navigating the Mississippi, should be now formally renewed.

The Americans were astounded; it seemed to them hardly worth while to have come so far to listen to such propositions. Concerning the proposed Indian pacification they had not even any powers, the United States being already busied in negotiating a treaty with the tribes as independent powers. The establishment of the neutral Indian belt was manifestly contrary to the established policy and obvious destiny of the nation. Neither was the answer agreeable, which was returned by Dr. Adams to the inquiry as to what was to be done with those citizens of the United States who had already settled in those parts of Michigan, Illinois, and Ohio, included within the territory which it was now proposed to make inalienably Indian. He said that these people, amounting perhaps to one hundred thousand, "must shift for themselves." The one-sided disarmament upon the lakes and along

the frontier was, by the understanding of all
nations, such an humiliation as is inflicted only
on a crushed adversary.   No return was offered
for the road between Halifax and Quebec ; nor
for the right of navigating the Mississippi.   The
treaty of peace of 1783, made in ignorance of the
topography of the unexplored northern country,
had established an impossible boundary line
running from the Lake of the Woods westward
along the forty-ninth parallel to the Mississippi ;
and as appurtenant to the British territory, thus
supposed to touch the river, a right of navigation
upon it was given.   It had since been discovered
that a line on that parallel would never touch
the Mississippi.   The same treaty had also
secured for the United States certain rights concerning the Northeastern fisheries.   The English
now insisted upon a re-affirmance of the privilege
given to them, without a re-affirmance of the
privilege given to the United States ; ignoring
the fact that the recent acquisition of Louisiana,
making the Mississippi wholly American, mate-
rially altered the propriety of a British right of
navigation upon it.

Apart from the intolerable character of these
demands, the personal bearing of the English
Commissioners did not tend to mitigate the
chagrin of the Americans.   The formal civil-
ities had counted with the American Commis-

sioners for more than they were worth, and had
induced them, in preparing a long dispatch to
the home government, to insert "a paragraph
complimentary to the personal deportment" of
the British. But before they sent off the document they revised it and struck out these
pleasant phrases. Not many days after the
first conference Mr. Adams notes that the tone
of the English Commissioners was even "more
peremptory, and their language more overbearing, than at the former conferences." A little
farther on he remarks that "the British note
is overbearing and insulting in its tone, like
the two former ones." Again he says : —

"The tone of all the British notes is arrogant,
overbearing, and offensive. The tone of ours is
neither so bold nor so spirited as I think it should
be. It is too much on the defensive, and too exces-
sive in the caution to say nothing irritating. I have
seldom been able to prevail upon my colleagues to
insert anything in the style of retort upon the harsh
and reproachful matter which we receive."

Many little passages-at-arms in the conferences are recited which amply bear out these
remarks as regards both parties. Perhaps,
however, it should be admitted that the Americans made up for the self-restraint which they
practised in conference by the disagreements
and bickerings in which they indulged when

consulting among themselves. Mr. Gallatin's serene temper and cool head were hardly taxed to keep the peace among his excited colleagues. Mr. Adams and Mr. Clay were especially prone to suspicions and to outbursts of anger. Mr. Adams often and candidly admits as much of himself, apparently not without good reason. At first the onerous task of drafting the numerous documents which the Commission had to present devolved upon him, a labor for which he was well fitted in all respects save, perhaps, a tendency to prolixity. He did not, however, succeed in satisfying his comrades, and the criticisms to which they subjected his composition galled his self-esteem severely, so much so that erelong he altogether relinquished this function, which was thereafter performed chiefly by Mr. Gallatin. As early as August 21, Mr. Adams says, not without evident bitterness, that though they all were agreed on the general view of the subject, yet in his "exposition of it, one objects to the form, another to the substance, of almost every paragraph." Mr. Gallatin would strike out everything possibly offensive to the Englishmen; Mr. Clay would draw his pen through every figurative expression; Mr. Russell, not content with agreeing to all the objections of both the others, would further amend the construction of every sentence;

and finally Mr. Bayard would insist upon writing all over again in his own language. All this nettled Mr. Adams exceedingly. On September 24 he again writes that it was agreed to adopt an article which he had drawn, " though with objections to almost every word " which he had used. " This," he says, " is a severity with which I alone am treated in our discussions by all my colleagues. Almost everything written by any of the rest is rejected, or agreed to with very little criticism, verbal or substantial. But every line that I write passes a gauntlet of objections by every one of my colleagues, which finally issues, for the most part, in the rejection of it all." He reflects, with a somewhat forced air of self-discipline, that this must indicate some faultiness in his composition which he must try to correct ; but in fact it is sufficiently evident that he was seldom persuaded that his papers were improved. Amid all this we see in the Diary many exhibitions of vexation. One day he acknowledges, " I cannot always restrain the irritability of my temper ; " another day he informed his colleagues, " with too much warmth, that they might be assured I was as determined as they were ; " again he reflects, " I, too, must not forget to keep a constant guard upon my temper, for the time is evidently approaching when it will be wanted." Mr. Gallatin alone seems not to have exasperated him; Mr. Clay and he were constantly in discussion, and often pretty hotly. Instead of coming nearer together, as time went on, these two fell farther apart. What Mr. Clay thought of Mr. Adams may probably be inferred from what we know that Mr. Adams thought of Mr. Clay. "Mr. Clay is losing his temper, and growing peevish and fractious," he writes on October 31; and constantly he repeats the like complaint. The truth is, that the precise New Englander and the impetuous Westerner were kept asunder not only by local interests but by habits and modes of thought utterly dissimilar. Some amusing glimpses of their private life illustrate this difference. Mr. Adams worked hard and diligently, allowing himself little leisure for pleasure; but Mr. Clay, without actually neglecting his duties, yet managed to find ample time for enjoyment. More than once Mr. Adams notes that, as he rose about five o'clock in the morning to light his own fire and begin the labors of the day by candle-light, he heard the parties breaking up and leaving Mr. Clay's rooms across the entry, where they had been playing cards all night long. In these little touches one sees the distinctive characters of the men well portrayed.

The very extravagance of the British de-

mands at least saved the Americans from per-
plexity. Mr. Clay, indeed, cherished an " in-
conceivable idea " that the Englishmen would
" finish by receding from the ground they had
taken ; " but meantime there could be no difference of opinion concerning the impossibility of
meeting them upon that ground.   Mr. Adams,
never lacking in courage, actually wished to
argue with them that it would be for the interests of Great Britain not less than of the
United States if Canada should be ceded to
the latter power.   Unfortunately his colleagues
would not support him in this audacious policy,
the humor of which is delicious.   It would have
been infinitely droll to see how the British Commissioners would have hailed such a proposition,
by way of appropriate termination of a conflict
in which the forces of their nation had captured and ransacked the capital city of the
Americans !

On August 21 the Englishmen invited the
Americans to dinner on the following Saturday.
" The chance is," wrote Mr. Adams, " that before that time the whole negotiation will be at
an end."   The banquet, however, did come off,
and a few more succeeded it ; feasts not marked
by any great geniality or warmth, except perhaps occasionally warmth of discussion.   So sure
were the Americans that they were about to

break off the negotiations that Mr. Adams began to consider by what route he should return
to St. Petersburg ; and they declined to renew
the tenure of their quarters for more than a few
days longer.   Like alarms were of frequent occurrence, even almost to the very day of agreement.   On September 15, at a dinner given by
the American Commissioners, Lord Gambier
asked Mr. Adams whether he would return immediately to St. Petersburg.   " Yes," replied
Mr. Adams, " that is, if you send us away."
His lordship " replied with assurances how
deeply he lamented it, and with a hope that we
should one day be friends again."   On the same
occasion Mr. Goulburn said that probably the
last note of the Americans would " terminate
the business," and that they " must fight it out."
Fighting it out was a much less painful prospect
for Great Britain just at that juncture than for
the United States, as the Americans realized
with profound anxiety.   " We so fondly cling
to the vain hope of peace, that every new proof
of its impossibility operates upon us as a disappointment," wrote Mr. Adams.   No amount
of pride could altogether conceal the fact that
the American Commissioners represented the
worsted party, and though they never openly
said so even among themselves, yet indirectly
they were obliged to recognize the truth.   On

November 10 we find Mr. Adams proposing to make concessions not permitted by their instructions, because, as he said: —

"I felt so sure that [the home government] would now gladly take the state before the war as the general basis of the peace, that I was prepared to take on me the responsibility of trespassing upon their instructions thus far. Not only so, but I would at this moment cheerfully give my life for a peace on this basis. If peace was possible, it would be on no other. I had indeed no hope that the proposal would be accepted."

Mr. Clay thought that the British would laugh at this: "They would say, Ay, ay! pretty fellows you, to think of getting out of the war as well as you got into it." This was not consoling for the representatives of that side which had declared war for the purpose of curing grievances and vindicating alleged rights. But that Mr. Adams correctly read the wishes of the government was proved within a very few days by the receipt of express authority from home "to conclude the peace on the basis of the *status ante bellum*." Three days afterwards, on November 27, three and a half months after the vexatious haggling had been begun, we encounter in the Diary the first real gleam of hope of a successful termination: "All the difficulties to the conclusion of a peace appear to be now so nearly removed, that my colleagues all consider it as certain. I myself think it probable."

There were, however, some three weeks more of negotiation to be gone through before the consummation was actually achieved, and the ill blood seemed to increase as the end was approached. The differences between the American Commissioners waxed especially serious concerning the fisheries and the navigation of the Mississippi. Mr. Adams insisted that if the treaty of peace had been so far abrogated by the war as to render necessary a re-affirmance of the British right of navigating the Mississippi, then a re-affirmance of the American rights in the Northeastern fisheries was equally necessary. This the English Commissioners denied. Mr. Adams said it was only an exchange of privileges presumably equivalent. Mr. Clay, however, was firmly resolved to prevent all stipulations admitting such a right of navigation, and the better to do so he was quite willing to let the fisheries go. The navigation privilege he considered "much too important to be conceded for the mere liberty of drying fish upon a desert," as he was pleased to describe a right for which the United States has often been ready to go to war and may yet some time do so. "Mr. Clay lost his temper," writes Mr.

Adams a day or two later, " as he generally
does whenever this right of the British to navi-
gate the Mississippi is discussed. He was utterly averse to admitting it as an equivalent for
a stipulation securing the contested part of the
fisheries. He said the more he heard of this
[the right of fishing], the more convinced he
was that it was of little or no value. He should
be glad to get it if he could, but he was sure
the British would not ultimately grant it. That
the navigation of the Mississippi, on the other
hand, was an object of immense importance,
and he could see no sort of reason for granting
it as an equivalent for the fisheries." Thus
spoke the representative of the West. The New
Englander — the son of the man whose exertions
had been chiefly instrumental in originally obtaining the grant of the Northeastern fishery
privileges — naturally went to the other extreme. He thought " the British right of navigating the Mississippi to be as nothing, considered as a grant from us. It was secured to them
by the peace of 1783, they had enjoyed it at the
commencement of the war, it had never been
injurious in the slightest degree to our own
people, and it appeared to [him] that the British claim to it was just and equitable." Further
he " believed the right to this navigation to be
a very useless thing to the British. . . . But

their national pride and honor were interested
in it; the government could not make a peace
which would abandon it." The fisheries, however, Mr. Adams regarded as one of the most
inestimable and inalienable of American rights.
It is evident that the United States could ill
have spared either Mr. Adams or Mr. Clay from
the negotiation, and the joinder of the two,
however fraught with discomfort to themselves,
well served substantial American interests.

Mr. Adams thought the British perfidious,
and suspected them of not entertaining any
honest intention of concluding a peace. On
December 12, after an exceedingly quarrelsome
conference, he records his belief that the British
have " insidiously kept open " two points, " for
the sake of finally breaking off the negotiations
and making all their other concessions proofs of
their extreme moderation, to put upon us the
blame of the rupture."

On December 11 we find Mr. Clay ready
" for a war three years longer," and anxious
" to begin to play at *brag* " with the Englishmen. His colleagues, more complaisant or having less confidence in their own skill in that
game, found it difficult to placate him; he
" stalked to and fro across the chamber, repeating five or six times, ' I will never sign a treaty
upon the *status ante bellum* with the Indian

article. So help me God!'" The next day
there was an angry controversy with the Englishmen.   The British troops had taken and held
Moose Island in Passamaquoddy Bay, the right-
ful ownership of which was in dispute.   The title
was to be settled by arbitrators.   But the question, whether the British should restore possession of the island pending the arbitration,
aroused bitter discussion.   " Mr. Goulburn and
Dr. Adams (the Englishman) immediately took
fire, and Goulburn lost all control of his temper.
He has always in such cases," says the Diary,
"a sort of convulsive agitation about him, and
the tone in which he speaks is more insulting
than the language which he uses."   Mr. Bayard
referred to the case of the Falkland Islands.
"'Why' (in a transport of rage), said Goulburn, 'in that case we sent a fleet and troops
and drove the fellows off; and that is what we
ought to have done in this case.'"   Mr. J. Q.
Adams, whose extensive and accurate information more than once annoyed his adversaries,
stated that, as he remembered it, " the Spaniards
in that case had driven the British off," — and
Lord Gambier helped his blundering colleague
out of the difficulty by suggesting a new subject, much as the defeated heroes of the Iliad
used to find happy refuge from death in a
god-sent cloud of dust.   It is amusing to read

that in the midst of such scenes as these the
show of courtesy was still maintained; and on
December 13 the Americans "all dined with
the British Plenipotentiaries," though "the
party was more than usually dull, stiff, and reserved." It was certainly forcing the spirit of
good fellowship. The next day Mr. Clay notified his colleagues that they were going "to
make a damned bad treaty, and he did not know
whether he would sign it or not;" and Mr.
Adams also said that he saw that the rest had
made up their minds "at last to yield the fishery point," in which case he also could not sign
the treaty. On the following day, however, the
Americans were surprised by receiving a note
from the British Commissioners, wherein they
made the substantial concession of omitting
from the treaty all reference to the fisheries and
the navigation of the Mississippi. But Mr.
Clay, on reading the note, "manifested some
chagrin," and "still talked of breaking off the
negotiation," even asking Mr. Adams to join
him in so doing, which request, however, Mr.
Adams very reasonably refused. Mr. Clay had
also been anxious to stand out for a distinct
abandonment of the alleged right of impressment; but upon this point he found none of his
colleagues ready to back him, and he was compelled perforce to yield. Agreement was there-

fore now substantially reached; a few minor matters were settled, and on December 24, 1814, the treaty was signed by all the eight negotiators.

It was an astonishing as well as a happy result. Never, probably, in the history of diplomacy has concord been produced from such discordant elements as had been brought together in Ghent. Dissension seemed to have become the mother of amity; and antipathies were mere preliminaries to a good understanding; in diplomacy as in marriage it had worked well to begin with a little aversion. But, in truth, this consummation was largely due to what had been going on in the English Cabinet. At the outset Lord Castlereagh had been very unwilling to conclude peace, and his disposition had found expression in the original intolerable terms prepared by the British Commissioners. But Lord Liverpool had been equally solicitous on the other side, and was said even to have tendered his resignation to the Prince Regent, if an accommodation should not be effected. His endeavors were fortunately aided by events in Europe. Pending the negotiations Lord Castlereagh went on a diplomatic errand to Vienna, and there fell into such threatening discussions with the Emperor of Russia and the King of Prussia, that he thought it

prudent to have done with the American war,
and wrote home pacific advices.   Hence, at last,
came such concessions as satisfied the Americans.

The treaty established " a firm and universal
peace between his Britannic Majesty and the
United States."   Each party was to restore all
captured territory, except that the islands of
which the title was in dispute were to remain
in the occupation of the party holding them at
the time of ratification until that title should be
settled by commissioners ; provision was made
also for the determination of all the open questions of boundary by sundry boards of commissioners ; each party was to make peace with
the Indian allies of the other.   Such were, in
substance, the only points touched upon by this
document.   Of the many subjects mooted between the negotiators scarcely any had survived the fierce contests which had been waged
concerning them.   The whole matter of the
navigation of the Mississippi, access to that
river, and a road through American territory,
had been dropped by the British ; while the
Americans had been well content to say nothing of the Northeastern fisheries, which they
regarded as still their own.   The disarmament
on the lakes and along the Canadian border,
and the neutralization of a strip of Indian

territory, were yielded by the English. The
Americans were content to have nothing said
about impressment; nor was any one of the
many illegal rights exercised by England formally abandoned. The Americans satisfied
themselves with the reflection that circumstances had rendered these points now only matters of abstract principle, since the pacification
of Europe had removed all opportunities and
temptations for England to persist in her previous objectionable courses. For the future it
was hardly to be feared that she would again
undertake to pursue a policy against which
it was evident that the United States were willing to conduct a serious war. There was, however, no provision for indemnification.

Upon a fair consideration, it must be admitted that though the treaty was silent upon
all the points which the United States had
made war for the purpose of enforcing, yet the
country had every reason to be gratified with
the result of the negotiation. The five Commissioners had done themselves ample credit.
They had succeeded in agreeing with each
other; they had avoided any fracture of a negotiation which, up to the very end, seemed
almost daily on the verge of being broken off
in anger; they had managed really to lose nothing, in spite of the fact that their side had

had decidedly the worst of the struggle. They had negotiated much more successfully than the armies of their countrymen had fought. The Marquis of Wellesley said, in the House of Lords, that "in his opinion the American Commissioners had shown a most astonishing superiority over the British during the whole of the correspondence." One cannot help wishing that the battle of New Orleans had taken place a little earlier, or that the negotiation had fallen a little later, so that news of that brilliant event could have reached the ears of the insolent Englishmen at Ghent, who had for three months been enjoying the malicious pleasure of lending to the Americans English newspapers containing accounts of American misfortunes. But that fortunate battle was not fought until a few days after the eight Commissioners had signed their compact. It is an interesting illustration of the slowness of communication which our forefathers had to endure, that the treaty crossed the Atlantic in a sailing ship in time to travel through much of the country simultaneously with the report of this farewell victory. Two such good pieces of news coming together set the people wild with delight. Even on the dry pages of Niles's "Weekly Register" occurs the triumphant paragraph: "Who would not be an American?

Long live the Republic! All hail! last asylum
of oppressed humanity! Peace is signed in the
arms of victory!" It was natural that most
of the ecstasy should be manifested concerning
the military triumph, and that the mass of the
people should find more pleasure in glorifying
General Jackson than in exalting the Commissioners. The value of their work, however, was
well proved by the voice of Great Britain. In
the London "Times" of December 30 appeared
a most angry tirade against the treaty, with
bitter sneers at those who called the peace an
"honorable" one. England, it was said, "had
attempted to force her principles on America,
and had failed." Foreign powers would say
that the English "had retired from the combat
with the stripes yet bleeding on their backs,
— with the recent defeats at Plattsburgh and
on Lake Champlain unavenged." The most
gloomy prognostications of further wars with
America when her naval power should have
waxed much greater were indulged. The loss
of prestige in Europe, "the probable loss of our
trans-Atlantic provinces," were among the results to be anticipated from this treaty into
which the English Commissioners had been be-
guiled by the Americans. These latter were
reviled with an abuse which was really the
highest compliment. The family name of Mr.

Adams gained no small access of distinction in England from this business.

After the conclusion of the treaty Mr. Adams went to Paris, and remained there until the middle of May, 1815, thus having the good fortune to witness the return of Napoleon and a great part of the events of the famous "hundred days." On May 26 he arrived in London, where there awaited him, in the hands of the Barings, his commission as Envoy Extraordinary and Minister Plenipotentiary to Great Britain. His first duty was, in connection with Mr. Clay and Mr. Gallatin, to negotiate a treaty of commerce, in which business he again met the same three British Commissioners by whom the negotiations at Ghent had been conducted, of whose abilities the government appeared to entertain a better opinion than the Marquis of Wellesley had expressed. This negotiation had been brought so far towards conclusion by his colleagues before his own arrival that Mr. Adams had little to do in assisting them to complete it. This little having been done, they departed and left him as Minister at the Court of St. James. Thus he fulfilled Washington's prophecy, by reaching the highest rank in the American diplomatic service.

Of his stay in Great Britain little need be said. He had few duties of importance to per-

form. The fisheries, the right of impressment,
and the taking away and selling of slaves by
British naval officers during the late war,
formed the subjects of many interviews between him and Lord Castlereagh, without, however, any definite results being reached. But
he succeeded in obtaining, towards the close of
his stay, some slight remission of the severe restrictions placed by England upon our trade
with her West Indian colonies. His relations
with a cabinet in which the principles of Castlereagh and Canning predominated could hardly
be cordial, yet he seems to have been treated
with perfect civility. Indeed, he was not a
man whom it was easy even for an Englishman
to insult. He remarks of Castlereagh, after
one of his first interviews with that nobleman:
"His deportment is sufficiently graceful, and
his person is handsome. His manner was cold,
but not absolutely repulsive." Before he left
he had the pleasure of having Mr. Canning
specially seek acquaintance with him. He met,
of course, many distinguished and many agreeable persons during his residence, and partook
of many festivities. especially of numerous civic
banquets at which toasts were formally given in
the dullest English fashion and he was obliged
to display his capacity for "table-cloth oratory,"
as he called it, more than was agreeable to him.

He was greatly bored by these solemn and pompous feedings. Partly in order to escape them he took a house at Ealing, and lived there during the greater part of his stay in England. "One of the strongest reasons for my remaining out of town," he writes, "is to escape the frequency of invitations at late hours, which consume so much precious time, and with the perpetually mortifying consciousness of inability to return the civility in the same manner." The republican simplicity, not to say poverty, forced upon American representatives abroad, was a very different matter in the censorious and unfriendly society of London from what it had been at the kindly disposed Court of St. Petersburg. The relationship between the mother country and the quondam colonies, especially at that juncture, was such as to render social life intolerably trying to an under-paid American minister.

Mr. Adams remained in England until June 15, 1817, when he sailed from Cowes, closing forever his long and honorable diplomatic career, and bidding his last farewell to Europe. He returned home to take the post of Secretary of State in the cabinet of James Monroe, then lately inaugurated as President of the United States.

CHAPTER II

SECRETARY OF STATE AND PRESIDENT

FROM the capitals of Russia and Great Britain to the capital of the United States was a striking change. Washington, in its early struggle for existence, was so unattractive a spot, that foreigners must have been at a loss to discover the principle which had governed the selection. It combined all the ugliness with all the discomfort of an unprosperous frontier settlement on an ill-chosen site. What must European diplomats have thought of a capital city where snakes two feet long invaded gentlemen's drawing-rooms, and a carriage, bringing home the guests from a ball, could be upset by the impenetrable depth of quagmire at the very door of a foreign minister's residence. A description of the city given by Mr. Mills, a Representative from Massachusetts, in 1815, is pathetic in its unutterable horror: —

"It is impossible [he writes] for me to describe to you my feelings on entering this miserable desert, this scene of desolation and horror. . . . My antici-

pations were almost infinitely short of the reality, and
I can truly say that the first appearance of this seat
of the national government has produced in me nothing but absolute loathing and disgust."

If the place wore such a dreadful aspect to
the simple denizen of a New England country
town, what must it have seemed to those who
were familiar with London and Paris? To
them the social life must have been scarcely
less dreary than the rest of the surroundings.
Accordingly, with this change of scene, the
Diary, so long a record of festivities sometimes dull and formal, but generally collecting
interesting and distinguished persons, ceases
almost wholly to refer to topics of society.
Yet, of course, even the foul streets could not
prevent people from occasionally meeting together. There were simple tea-drinkings, stupid weekly dinners at the President's, infre-
quent receptions by Mrs. Monroe, card-parties
and conversation-parties, which at the British
minister's were very " elegant," and at the
French minister's were more gay. Mons. de
Neuville, at his dinners, used to puzzle and
astound the plain-living Yankees by serving
dishes of " turkeys without bones, and pud-
dings in the form of fowls, fresh cod disguised
like a salad, and celery like oysters ; " further,
he scandalized some and demoralized others by

having dancing on Saturday evenings, which
the New England ladies had been "educated to
consider as holy time." Mr. and Mrs. Adams
used to give weekly parties on Tuesday evenings, and apparently many persons stood not a
little in awe of these entertainments and of
the givers of them, by reason of their superior
familiarity with the manners and customs of
the best society of Europe. Mrs. Adams was,
"on the whole, a very pleasant and agreeable
woman ; but the Secretary [had] no talent to
entertain a mixed company, either by conversation or manners ; " thus writes this same Mr.
Mills, whose sentiments towards Mr. Adams
were those of respect rather than of personal
liking. The favorite dissipation then consisted
in card-playing, and the stakes were too often
out of all just proportion to the assets of the
gamesters. At one time Mr. Clay was reputed
to have lost $8,000, an amount so considerable
for him as to weigh upon his mind to the manifest detriment of his public functions. But
sometimes the gentlemen resident in the capital
met for purposes less innocent than Saturday
evening cotillons, or even than extravagant bet-
ting at the card-table, and stirred the dulness
of society by a duel. Mr. Adams tells of one
affair of this sort, fought between ex-Senator
Mason, of Virginia, and his cousin, wherein the

weapons used were muskets, and the distance
was only six paces. Mason was killed; his
cousin was wounded, and only by a lucky accident escaped with his life. Mr. Adams had
little time and less taste for either the amuse-
ments or the dangers thus offered to him; he
preferred to go to bed in good season, to get up
often long before daybreak, and to labor assiduously the livelong day. His favorite exercise
was swimming in the Potomac, where he accomplished feats which would have been extraordinary for a young and athletic man.

The most important, perplexing, and time-
consuming duties then called for by the condition of public affairs happened to fall within
Mr. Adams's department. Monroe's administration has been christened the "era of good
feeling;" and, so far as political divisions
among the people at large were concerned, this
description is correct enough. There were no
great questions of public policy dividing the
nation. There could hardly be said to be two
political parties. With the close of the war
the malcontent Federalists had lost the only
substantial principle upon which they had been
able vigorously to oppose the administration,
and as a natural consequence the party rapidly
shrank to insignificant proportions, and became
of hardly more importance than were the Jac-

obites in England after their last hopes had
been quenched by the failure of the Rebellion
of '45. The Federalist faith, like Jacobitism,
lingered in a few neighborhoods, and was maintained by a few old families, who managed to
associate it with a sense of their own pride and
dignity ; but as an effective opposition or influential party organization it was effete, and
no successor was rising out of its ruins. In a
broad way, therefore, there was political harmony to a very remarkable degree.

But among individuals there was by no means
a prevailing good feeling. Not held together by
the pressure exerted by the antagonism of a
strong hostile force, the prominent men of the
Cabinet and in Congress were busily employed
in promoting their own individual interests.
Having no great issues with which to identify
themselves, and upon which they could openly
and honorably contend for the approval of the
nation, their only means for securing their re-
spective private ends lay in secretly overreach-
ing and supplanting each other. Infinite skill
was exerted by each to inveigle his rival into
an unpopular position or a compromising light.
By a series of precedents Mr. Adams, as Secretary of State, appeared most prominent as a
candidate for the succession to the Presidency.
But Mr. Crawford, in the Treasury Department,

had been very near obtaining the nomination instead of Monroe, and he was firmly resolved to
secure it so soon as Mr. Monroe's eight years
should have elapsed. He, therefore, finding
much leisure left upon his hands by the not
very exacting business of his office, devoted his
ingenuity to devising schemes for injuring the
prestige of Mr. Adams. Mr. Clay also had
been greatly disappointed that he had not been
summoned to be Secretary of State, and so
made heir apparent. His personal enmity was
naturally towards Mr. Monroe; his political
enmity necessarily also included Mr. Adams,
whose appointment he had privately sought to
prevent. He therefore at once set himself assiduously to oppose and thwart the administration, and to make it unsuccessful and unpopular. That Clay was in the main and upon all
weighty questions an honest statesman and a
real patriot must be admitted, but just at this
period no national crisis called his nobler qualities into action, and his course was largely influenced by selfish considerations. It was not
long before Mr. Calhoun also entered the lists,
though in a manner less discreditable to himself, personally, than were the resources of
Crawford and Clay. The daily narrations and
comments of Mr. Adams display and explain
in a manner highly instructive, if not altogether

Wm. H. Crawford

agreeable, the ambitions and the manœuvres, the hollow alliances and unworthy intrigues, not only of these three, but also of many other estimable gentlemen then in political life. The difference between those days and our own seems not so great as the *laudatores temporis acti* are wont to proclaim it. The elaborate machinery which has since been constructed was then unknown; rivals relied chiefly upon their own astuteness and the aid of a few personal friends and adherents for carrying on contests and attaining ends which are now sought by vastly more complex methods. What the stage-coach of that period was to the railroads of to-day, or what the hand-loom was to our great cotton mills, such also was the political intriguing of cabinet ministers, senators, and representatives to our present party machinery. But the temper was no better, honor was no keener, the sense of public duty was little more disinterested then than now. One finds no serious traces of vulgar financial dishonesty recorded in these pages, in which Mr. Adams has handed down the political life of the second and third decades of our century with a photographic accuracy. But one does not see a much higher level of faithfulness to ideal standards in political life than now exists.

As has been said, it so happened that in Mr.

Monroe's administration the heaviest burden of
labor and responsibility rested upon Mr. Adams;
the most important and most perplexing questions fell within his department. Domestic
breaches had been healed, but foreign breaches
gaped with threatening jaws. War with Spain
seemed imminent. Her South American colonies
were then waging their contest for independence,
and naturally looked to the late successful rebels
of the northern continent for acts of neighborly
sympathy and good fellowship. Their efforts to
obtain official recognition and the exchange of
ministers with the United States were eager and
persistent. Privateers fitted out at Baltimore
gave the State Department scarcely less cause
for anxiety than the shipbuilders of Liverpool
gave to the English Cabinet in 1863–64. These
perplexities, as is well known, caused the passage
of the first " Neutrality Act," which first formulated and has since served to establish the
principle of international obligation in such
matters, and has been the basis of all subsequent
legislation upon the subject not only in this
country but also in Great Britain.

The European powers, impelled by a natural
distaste for rebellion by colonists, and also believing that Spain would in time prevail over
the insurgents, turned a deaf ear to South American agents. But in the United States it was

different. Here it was anticipated that the revolted communities were destined to win; Mr.
Adams records this as his own opinion; besides
which there was also a natural sympathy felt
by our people in such a conflict in their own
quarter of the globe. Nevertheless, in many
anxious cabinet discussions, the President and
the Secretary of State established the policy of
reserve and caution. Rebels against an established government are like plaintiffs in litiga-
tion; the burden of proof is upon them, and the
neutral nations who are a sort of quasi-jurors
must not commit themselves to a decision prematurely. The grave and inevitable difficulties
besetting the administration in this matter were
seriously enhanced by the conduct of Mr. Clay.
Seeking nothing so eagerly as an opportunity to
harass the government, he could have found none
more to his taste than this question of South
American recognition. His enthusiastic and
rhetorical temperament rejoiced in such a topic
for his luxuriant oratory, and he lauded freedom
and abused the administration with a force
of expression far from gratifying to the responsible heads of government in their troublesome
task.

Apart from these matters the United States
had direct disputes of a threatening character
pending with Spain concerning the boundaries

of Louisiana.   Naturally enough boundary lines
in the half explored wilderness of this vast continent were not then marked with that indis-
putable accuracy which many generations and
much bloodshed had achieved in Europe; and
of all uncertain boundaries that of Louisiana
was the most so.   Area enough to make two or
three States, more or less, might or might not
be included therein.   Such doubts had proved
a ready source of quarrel, which could hardly
be assuaged by General Jackson marching about
in unquestionable Spanish territory, seizing
towns and hanging people after his lawless,
ignorant, energetic fashion.   Mr. Adams's chief
labor, therefore, was by no means of a promising character, being nothing less difficult than
to conclude a treaty between enraged Spain and
the rapacious United States, where there was so
much wrong and so much right on both sides,
and such a wide obscure realm of doubt between
the two that an amicable agreement might well
seem not only beyond expectation but beyond
hope.

Many and various also were the incidental
obstacles in Mr. Adams's way.   Not the least
lay in the ability of Don Onis, the Spanish
Minister, an ambassador well selected for his
important task and whom the American thus
described : —

"Cold, calculating, wily, always commanding his own temper, proud because he is a Spaniard, but supple and cunning, accommodating the tone of his pretensions precisely to the degree of endurance of his opponent, bold and overbearing to the utmost extent to which it is tolerated, careless of what he asserts or how grossly it is proved to be unfounded, his morality appears to be that of the Jesuits as exposed by Pascal. He is laborious, vigilant, and ever attentive to his duties; a man of business and of the world."

Fortunately this so dangerous negotiator was hardly less anxious than Mr. Adams to conclude a treaty. Yet he, too, had his grave difficulties to encounter. Spanish arrogance had not declined with the decline of Spanish strength, and the concessions demanded from that ancient monarchy by the upstart republic seemed at once exasperating and humiliating. The career of Jackson in Florida, while it exposed the weakness of Spain, also sorely wounded her pride. Nor could the grandees, three thousand miles away, form so accurate an opinion of the true condition and prospects of affairs as could Don Onis upon this side of the water. One day, begging Mr. Adams to meet him upon a question of boundary, "he insisted much upon the infinite pains he had taken to prevail upon his government to come to terms of accommodation," and pathetically declared that "the King's Council was composed of such ignorant and stupid *nigauds*, grandees of Spain, and priests," that Mr. Adams "could have no conception of their obstinacy and imbecility."

Other difficulties in Mr. Adams's way were such as ought not to have been encountered. The only substantial concession which he was willing to make was in accepting the Sabine instead of the Rio del Norte as the southwestern boundary of Louisiana. But no sooner did rumors of this possible yielding get abroad than he was notified that Mr. Clay "would take ground against" any treaty embodying it. From Mr. Crawford a more dangerous and insidious policy was to be feared. Presumably he would be well pleased either to see Mr. Adams fail altogether in the negotiation, or to see him conclude a treaty which would be in some essential feature odious to the people.

"That all his conduct [wrote Mr. Adams] is governed by his views to the Presidency, as the ultimate successor to Mr. Monroe, and that his hopes depend upon a result unfavorable to the success or at least to the popularity of the Administration, is perfectly clear. . . . His talent is intrigue. And as it is in the foreign affairs that the success or failure of the Administration will be most conspicuous, and as their success would promote the reputation and in-

fluence, and their failure would lead to the disgrace
of the Secretary of State, Crawford's personal views
centre in the ill-success of the Administration in its
foreign relations ; and, perhaps unconscious of his
own motives, he will always be impelled to throw
obstacles in its way, and to bring upon the Department of State especially any feeling of public dissatisfaction that he can, . . . and although himself a
member of the Administration, he perceives every
day more clearly that his only prospect of success
hereafter depends upon the failure of the Administration by measures of which he must take care to
make known his disapprobation."

President Monroe was profoundly anxious for
the consummation of the treaty, and though for
a time he was in perfect accord with Mr. Adams,
yet as the Spanish minister gradually drew
nearer and nearer to a full compliance with the
American demands, Monroe began to fear that
the Secretary would carry his unyielding habit
too far, and by insistence upon extreme points
which might well enough be given up, would
allow the country to drift into war.

Fortunately, as it turned out, Mr. Adams was
not afraid to take the whole responsibility of
success or failure upon his own shoulders, showing indeed a high and admirable courage and
constancy amid such grave perplexities, in which
it seemed that all his future political fortunes

were involved. He caused the proffered mediation of Great Britain to be rejected. He availed
himself of no aid save only the services of
Mons. de Neuville, the French minister, who
took a warm interest in the negotiation, ex-
postulated and argued constantly with Don
Onis and sometimes with Mr. Adams, served as
a channel of communication and carried messages, propositions, and denials, which could
better come filtered through a neutral go-between than pass direct from principal to principal. In fact, Mr. Adams needed no other kind
of aid except just this which was so readily
furnished by the civil and obliging Frenchman.
As if he had been a mathematician solving a
problem in dynamics, he seemed to have measured the precise line to which the severe pressure of Spanish difficulties would compel Don
Onis to advance. This line he drew sharply,
and taking his stand upon it in the beginning
he made no important alterations in it to the
end. Day by day the Spaniard would reluctantly approach toward him at one point or another, solemnly protesting that he could not
make another move, by argument and entreaty
urging, almost imploring, Mr. Adams in turn to
advance and meet him. But Mr. Adams stood
rigidly still, sometimes not a little vexed by the
other's lingering manœuvres, and actually once

saying to the courtly Spaniard that he "was so wearied out with the discussion that it had become nauseous;" and, again, that he "really could discuss no longer, and had given it up in despair." Yet all the while he was never wholly free from anxiety concerning the accuracy of his calculations as to how soon the Don might on his side also come to a final stand. Many a tedious and alarming pause there was, but after each halt progress was in time renewed. At last the consummation was reached, and except in the aforementioned matter of the Sabine boundary no concession even in details had been made by Mr. Adams. The United States was to receive Florida, and in return only agreed to settle the disputed claims of certain of her citizens against Spain to an amount not to exceed five million dollars; while the claims of Spanish subjects against the United States were wholly expunged. The western boundary was so established as to secure for this country the much-coveted outlet to the shores of the "South Sea," as the Pacific Ocean was called, south of the Columbia River; the line also was run along the southern banks of the Red and Arkansas rivers, leaving all the islands to the United States and precluding Spain from the right of navigation. Mr. Adams had achieved a great triumph.

On February 22, 1819, the two negotiators

signed and sealed the counterparts of the treaty. Mr. Adams notes that it is " perhaps the most important day of my life," and justly called it " a great epoch in our history." Yet on the next day the " Washington City Gazette " came out with a strong condemnation of the Sabine concession, and expressed the hope that the Senate would not agree to it. " This paragraph," said Mr. Adams, " comes directly or indirectly from Mr. Clay." But the paragraph did no harm, for on the following day the treaty was confirmed by an unanimous vote of the Senate.

It was not long, however, before the pleasure justly derivable from the completion of this great labor was cruelly dashed. It appeared that certain enormous grants of land, made by the Spanish king to three of his nobles, and which were supposed to be annulled by the treaty, so that the territory covered by them would become the public property of the United States, bore date earlier than had been understood, and for this reason would, by the terms of the treaty, be left in full force. This was a serious matter, and such steps as were still possible to set it right were promptly taken. Mr. Adams appealed to Don Onis to state in writing that he himself had understood that these grants were to be annulled, and that such had been the intention of the treaty. The Spaniard replied in a shape imperfectly satisfactory. He shuffled, evaded, and laid himself open to suspicion of unfair dealing, though the charge could not be regarded as fully proved against him. Mr. Adams, while blaming himself for carelessness in not having more closely examined original documents, yet felt " scarce a doubt " that Onis " did intend by artifice to cover the grants while we were under the undoubting impression they were annulled ; " and he said to M. de Neuville, concerning this dark transaction, that " it was not the ingenious device of a public minister, but ' *une fourberie de Scapin.*' " Before long the rumor got abroad in the public prints in the natural shape of a " malignant distortion," and Mr. Adams was compelled to see with chagrin his supposed brilliant success threatening to turn actually to his grave discredit by reason of this unfortunate oversight.

What might have been the result had the treaty been ratified by Spain can only be surmised. But it so befell — happily enough for the United States and for Mr. Adams, as it afterwards turned out — that the Spanish government refused to ratify. The news was, however, that they would forthwith dispatch a new minister to explain this refusal and to renew negotiations.

For his own private part Mr. Adams strove

to endure this buffet of unkindly fortune with
that unflinching and stubborn temper, slightly
dashed with bitterness, which stood him in good
stead in many a political trial during his hard-
fighting career. But in his official capacity he
had also to consider and advise what it be-
hooved the administration to do under the circumstances. The feeling was widespread that
the United States ought to possess Florida, and
that Spain had paltered with us long enough.
More than once in cabinet meetings during the
negotiation the Secretary of State, who was always prone to strong measures, had expressed
a wish for an act of Congress authorizing the
Executive to take forcible possession of Florida
and of Galveston in the event of Spain refusing
to satisfy the reasonable demands made upon
her. Now, stimulated by indignant feeling, his
prepossession in favor of vigorous action was
greatly strengthened, and his counsel was that
the United States should prepare at once to
take and hold the disputed territory, and indeed
some undisputed Spanish territory also. But
Mr. Monroe and the rest of the Cabinet preferred a milder course; and France and Great
Britain ventured to express to this country a
hope that no violent action would be precipi-
tately taken. So the matter lay by for a while,
awaiting the coming of the promised envoy
from Spain.

At this time the great question of the admission of Missouri into the Union of States began to agitate Congress and the nation. Mr. Adams, deeply absorbed in the perplexing affairs of his department, into which this domestic problem did not enter, was at first careless of it. His ideas concerning the matter, he wrote, were a " chaos ; " but it was a " chaos " into which his interest in public questions soon compelled him to bring order. In so doing he for the first time fairly exposes his intense repulsion for slavery, his full appreciation of the irrepressible character of the conflict between the slave and the free populations, and the sure tendency of that conflict to a dissolution of the Union. Few men at that day read the future so clearly. While dissolution was generally regarded as a threat not really intended to be carried out, and compromises were supposed to be amply sufficient to control the successive emergencies, the underlying moral force of the anti-slavery movement acting against the encroaching necessities of the slave-holding communities constituted an element and involved possibilities which Mr. Adams, from his position of observation outside the immediate controversy, noted with foreseeing accuracy. He discerned in passing events the " title-page to a great tragic volume ; " and he predicted that the more or less distant but

sure end must be an attempt to dissolve the
Union. His own position was distinctly defined
from the outset, and his strong feelings were
vigorously expressed. He beheld with profound
regret the superiority of the slave-holding party
in ability; he remarked sadly how greatly they
excelled in debating power their lukewarm opponents; he was filled with indignation against
the Northern men of Southern principles. "Slavery," he wrote, "is the great and foul stain
upon the North American Union, and it is a
contemplation worthy of the most exalted soul
whether its total abolition is or is not practicable." "A life devoted to" the emancipation
problem "would be nobly spent or sacrificed."
He talks with much acerbity of expression about
the "slave-drivers," and the "flagrant image of
human inconsistency" presented by men who
had "the Declaration of Independence on their
lips and the merciless scourge of slavery in their
hands." "Never," he says, "since human sentiments and human conduct were influenced by
human speech was there a theme for eloquence
like the free side of this question. . . . Oh, if
but one man could arise with a genius capable
of comprehending, and an utterance capable of
communicating those eternal truths that belong
to this question, to lay bare in all its nakedness
that outrage upon the goodness of God, human

slavery; now is the time and this is the occasion, upon which such a man would perform the duties of an angel upon earth." Before the Abolitionists had begun to preach their great crusade this was strong and ardent language for a statesman's pen. Nor were these exceptional passages; there is much more of the same sort at least equally forcible. Mr. Adams notes an interesting remark made to him by Calhoun at this time. The great Southern chief, less prescient than Mr. Adams, declared that he did not think that the slavery question " would produce a dissolution of the Union; but if it should, the South would be from necessity compelled to form an alliance offensive and defensive with Great Britain."

Concerning a suggestion that civil war might be preferable to the extension of slavery beyond the Mississippi, Adams said : " This is a question between the rights of human nature and the Constitution of the United States " — a form of stating the case which leaves no doubt concerning his ideas of the intrinsic right and wrong in the matter. His own notion was that slavery could not be got rid of within the Union, but that the only method would be dissolution, after which he trusted that the course of events would in time surely lead to reorganization upon the basis of universal freedom for all.

He was not a disunionist in any sense, yet it is evident that his strong tendency and inclination were to regard emancipation as a weight in the scales heavier than union, if it should ever come to the point of an option between the two.

Strangely enough the notion of a forcible retention of the slave States within the Union does not seem to have been at this time a substantial element of consideration. Mr. Adams acknowledged that there was no way at once of preserving the Union and escaping from the present emergency save through the door of compromise. He maintained strenuously the power of Congress to prohibit slavery in the Territories, and denied that either Congress or a state government could establish slavery as a new institution in any State in which it was not already existing and recognized by law.

This agitation of the slavery question made itself felt in a way personally interesting to Mr. Adams, by the influence it was exerting upon men's feelings concerning the still pending and dubious treaty with Spain. The South became anxious to lay hands upon the Floridas and upon as far-reaching an area as possible in the direction of Mexico, in order to carve it up into more slave States ; the North, on the other hand, no longer cared very eagerly for an extension of the Union upon its southern side. Sectional in-

terests were getting to be more considered than
national. Mr. Adams could not but recognize
that in the great race for the Presidency, in
which he could hardly help being a competitor,
the chief advantage which he seemed to have
won when the Senate unanimously ratified the
Spanish treaty, had almost wholly vanished
since that treaty had been repudiated by Spain
and was now no longer desired by a large proportion of his own countrymen.

Matters stood thus when the new Spanish
envoy, Vivês, arrived. Other elements, which
there is not space to enumerate here, besides
those referred to, now entering newly into the
state of affairs, further reduced the improba-
bility of agreement almost to hopelessness. Mr.
Adams, despairing of any other solution than
a forcible seizure of Florida, to which he had
long been far from averse, now visibly relaxed
his efforts to meet the Spanish negotiator. Perhaps no other course could have been more
effectual in securing success than this obvious
indifference to it. In the prevalent condition
of public feeling and of his own sentiments Mr.
Adams easily assumed towards General Vivês a
decisive bluntness, not altogether consonant to
the habits of diplomacy, and manifested an un-
changeable stubbornness which left no room for
discussion. His position was simply that Spain

might make such a treaty as the United States
demanded, or might take the consequences of
her refusal.   His dogged will wore out the
Spaniard's pride, and after a fruitless delay the
King and Cortes ratified the treaty in its original shape, with the important addition of an
explicit annulment of the land grants.   It was
again sent in to the Senate, and in spite of the
" continued, systematic, and laborious effort " of
" Mr. Clay and his partisans to make it unpopular," it was ratified by a handsome majority,
there being against it " only four votes — Brown,
of Louisiana, who married a sister of Clay's
wife ; Richard M. Johnson, of Kentucky, against
his own better judgment, from mere political
subserviency to Clay ; Williams, of Tennessee,
from party impulses connected with hatred of
General Jackson ; and Trimble, of Ohio, from
some maggot of the brain."   Two years had
elapsed since the former ratification, and no
little patience had been required to await so
long the final achievement of a success so ar-
dently longed for, once apparently gained, and
anon so cruelly thwarted.   But the triumph was
rather enhanced than diminished by all this difficulty and delay.   A long and checkered history, wherein appeared infinite labor, many a
severe trial of temper and hard test of moral
courage, bitter disappointment, ignoble artifices

of opponents, ungenerous opposition growing
out of unworthy personal motives at home, was
now at last closed by a chapter which appeared
only the more gratifying by contrast with what
had gone before. Mr. Adams recorded, with
less of exultation than might have been pardon-
able, the utter discomfiture of " all the calcula-
tors of my downfall by the Spanish negotiation,"
and reflected cheerfully that he had been left
with " credit rather augmented than impaired
by the result," — credit not in excess of his deserts. Many years afterwards, in changed circumstances, an outcry was raised against the
agreement which was arrived at concerning the
southwestern boundary of Louisiana. Most
unjustly it was declared that Mr. Adams had
sacrificed a portion of the territory of the United
States. But political motives were too plainly
to be discerned in these tardy criticisms; and
though General Jackson saw fit, for personal
reasons, to animadvert severely upon the clause
establishing this boundary line, yet there was
abundant evidence to show not only that he,
like almost everybody else, had been greatly
pleased with it at the time, but even that he
had then upon consultation expressed a deliberate and special approval.

The same day, February 22, 1821, closed,
says Mr. Adams, " two of the most memorable

transactions of my life." That he should speak
thus of the exchange of ratifications of the
Spanish treaty is natural; but the other so
"memorable transaction" may not appear of
equal magnitude. It was the sending in to Congress of his report upon weights and measures.
This was one of those vast labors, involving
tenfold more toil than all the negotiations with
Onis and Vivês, but bringing no proportionate
fame, however well it might be performed. The
subject was one which had "occupied for the
last sixty years many of the ablest men in
Europe, and to which all the power and all the
philosophical and mathematical learning and ingenuity of France and of Great Britain" had
during that period been incessantly directed.
It was fairly enough described as a "fearful and
oppressive task." Upon its dry and uncongenial difficulties Mr. Adams had been employed
with his wonted industry for upwards of four
years; he now spoke of the result modestly as
"a hurried and imperfect work." But others,
who have had to deal with the subject, have
found this report a solid and magnificent monument of research and reflection, which has not
even yet been superseded by later treatises. Mr.
Adams was honest in labor as in everything,
and was never careless at points where inaccuracy or lack of thoroughness might be ex-

pected to escape detection. Hence his success
in a task upon which it is difficult to imagine
other statesmen of that day — Clay, Webster,
or Calhoun, for example — so much as making
an effort. The topic is not one concerning
which readers would tolerate much lingering.
Suffice it then to say that the document illustrated the ability and the character of the man,
and so with this brief mention to dismiss in a
paragraph an achievement which, had it been
accomplished in any more showy department,
would alone have rendered Mr. Adams famous.

It is highly gratifying now to look back upon
the high spirit and independent temper uniformly displayed by Mr. Adams abroad and at
home in all dealings with foreign powers. Never
in any instance did he display the least tinge
of that rodomontade and boastful extravagance
which have given an underbred air to so many
of our diplomats, and which inevitably cause the
basis for such self-laudation to appear of dubious
sufficiency. But he had the happy gift of a native pride which enabled him to support in the
most effective manner the dignity of the people
for whom he spoke. For example, in treaties between the United States and European powers
the latter were for a time wont to name themselves first throughout the instruments, contrary
to the custom of alternation practised in trea-

ties between themselves. With some difficulty, partly interposed, it must be confessed, by his own American coadjutors, Mr. Adams succeeded in putting a stop to this usage.   It was a matter of insignificant detail, in one point of view ; but in diplomacy insignificant details often symbolize important facts, and there is no question that this habit had been construed as a tacit but intentional arrogance of superiority on the part of the Europeans.

For a long period after the birth of the country there was a strong tendency, not yet so eradicated as to be altogether undiscoverable, on the part of American statesmen to keep one eye turned covertly askance upon the trans-Atlantic courts, and to consider, not without a certain anxious deference, what appearance the new United States might be presenting to the critical eyes of foreign countries and diplomats. Mr. Adams was never guilty of such indirect admissions of an inferiority which apparently he never felt.   In the matter of the acquisition of Florida, Crawford suggested that England and France regarded the people of the United States as ambitious and encroaching ; wherefore he advised a moderate policy in order to remove this impression. Mr. Adams on the other side declared that he was not in favor of our giving ourselves any concern whatever about the opinions of any foreign power. "If the world do not hold us for Romans," he said, "they will take us for Jews, and of the two vices I would rather be charged with that which has greatness mingled in its composition." His views were broad and grand. He was quite ready to have the world become "familiarized with the idea of considering our proper dominion to be the continent of North America." This extension he declared to be a "law of nature." To suppose that Spain and England could, through the long lapse of time, retain their possessions on this side of the Atlantic seemed to him a "physical, moral, and political absurdity."

The doctrine which has been christened with the name of President Monroe seems likely to win for him the permanent glory of having originated the wise policy which that familiar phrase now signifies. It might, however, be shown that by right of true paternity the bantling should have borne a different patronymic. Not only is the "Monroe Doctrine," as that phrase is customarily construed in our day, much more comprehensive than the simple theory first expressed by Monroe and now included in the modern doctrine as a part in the whole, but a principle more fully identical with the imperial one of to-day had been conceived and

shaped by Mr. Adams before the delivery of
Monroe's famous message. As has just been
remarked, he looked forward to the possession
of the whole North American continent by the
United States as a sure destiny, and for his own
part, whenever opportunity offered, he was never
backward to promote this glorious ultimate consummation. He was in favor of the acquisition
of Louisiana, whatever fault he might find with
the scheme of Mr. Jefferson for making it a
state; he was ready in 1815 to ask the British
plenipotentiaries to cede Canada simply as a
matter of common sense and mutual conven-
ience, and as the comfortable result of a war
in which the United States had been worsted;
he never labored harder than in negotiating for
the Floridas, and in pushing our western boundaries to the Pacific; in April, 1823, he wrote
to the American minister at Madrid the significant remark: " It is scarcely possible to resist
the conviction that the annexation of Cuba to
our Federal Republic will be indispensable to
the continuance and integrity of the Union."
Encroachments never seemed distasteful to him,
and he was always forward to stretch a point
in order to advocate or defend a seizure of disputed North American territory, as in the cases
of Amelia Island, Pensacola, and Galveston.
When discussion arose with Russia concerning

her possessions on the northwest coast of this continent, Mr. Adams audaciously told the Russian minister, Baron Tuyl, July 17, 1823, "that we should contest the rights of Russia to *any* territorial establishment on this continent, and that we should assume distinctly the principle that the American continents are no longer subjects for any new European colonial establishments." "This," says Mr. Charles Francis Adams in a footnote to the passage in the Diary, "is the first hint of the policy so well known afterwards as the Monroe Doctrine." Nearly five months later, referring to the same matter in his message to Congress, December 2, 1823, President Monroe said: "The occasion has been judged proper for asserting, as a principle in which the rights and interests of the United States are involved, that the American continents, by the free and independent condition which they have assumed and maintain, are henceforth not to be considered as subjects for future colonization by any European powers."

It will be observed that both Mr. Adams and President Monroe used the phrase "continents," including thereby South as well as North America. A momentous question was imminent, which fortunately never called for a determination by action, but which in this latter part of 1823 threatened to do so at any moment.

Cautious and moderate as the United States
had been, under Mr. Adams's guidance, in recognizing the freedom and autonomy of the South
American states, yet in time the recognition
was made of one after another, and the emancipation of South America had come, while Mr.
Adams was yet Secretary, to be regarded as an
established fact. But now, in 1823–24, came
mutterings from across the Atlantic indicating
a strong probability that the members of the
Holy Alliance would interfere in behalf of mo-
narchical and anti-revolutionary principles, and
would assist in the resubjugation of the successful insurgents. That each one of the powers who should contribute to this huge crusade
would expect and receive territorial reward
could not be doubted. Mr. Adams, in unison
with most of his countrymen, contemplated with
profound distrust and repulsion the possibility
of such an European inroad. Stimulated by
the prospect of so unwelcome neighbors, he
prepared some dispatches, "drawn to corre-
spond exactly" with the sentiments of Mr.
Monroe's message, in which he appears to have
taken a very high and defiant position. These
documents, coming before the Cabinet for consideration, caused some flutter among his associates. In the possible event of the Holy Alliance actually intermeddling in South American

affairs, it was said, the principles enunciated by the Secretary of State would involve this country in war with a very formidable confederation. Mr. Adams acknowledged this, but courageously declared that in such a crisis he felt quite ready to take even this spirited stand. His audacious spirit went far in advance of the cautious temper of the Monroe administration; possibly it went too far in advance of the dictates of a wise prudence, though fortunately the course of events never brought this question to trial; and it is at least gratifying to contemplate such a manifestation of daring temper.

But though so bold and independent, Mr. Adams was not habitually reckless nor prone to excite animosity by needless arrogance in action or extravagance in principle. In any less perilous extremity than was presented by this menaced intrusion of combined Europe he followed rigidly the wise rule of non-interference. For many years before this stage was reached he had been holding in difficult check the enthusiasts who, under the lead of Mr. Clay, would have embroiled us with Spain and Portugal. Once he was made the recipient of a very amusing proposition from the Portuguese minister, that the United States and Portugal, as "the two great powers of the western hemisphere," should concert together a grand American system. The drollery of this notion was of a kind that Mr. Adams could appreciate, though to most manifestations of humor he was utterly impervious. But after giving vent to some contemptuous merriment he adds, with a just and serious pride: " As to an American system, we have it ; we constitute the whole of it ; there is no community of interests or of principles between North and South America." This sound doctrine was put forth in 1820; and it was only modified in the manner that we have seen during a brief period in 1823, in face of the alarming vision not only of Spain and Portugal restored to authority, but of Russia in possession of California and more, France in possession of Mexico, and perhaps Great Britain becoming mistress of Cuba.

So far as European affairs were concerned, Mr. Adams always and consistently refused to become entangled in them, even in the slightest and most indirect manner. When the cause of Greek liberty aroused the usual throng of noisy advocates for active interference, he contented himself with expressions of cordial sympathy, accompanied by perfectly distinct and explicit statements that under no circumstances could any aid in the way of money or auxiliary forces be expected from this country. Neutrals

we were and would remain in any and all
European quarrels. When Stratford Canning
urged, with the uttermost measure of persistence of which even he was capable, that for
the suppression of the slave trade some such arrangement might be made as that of mixed tribunals for the trial of slave-trading vessels, and
alleged that divers European powers were unit-
ing for this purpose, Mr. Adams suggested, as
an insuperable obstacle, "the general extra-Eu-
ropean policy of the United States — a policy which they had always pursued as best
suited to their own interests, and best adapted
to harmonize with those of Europe. This policy had also been that of Europe, which had
never considered the United States as belonging to her system. . . . It was best for both
parties that they should continue to do so." In
any European combinations, said Mr. Adams,
in which the United States should become a
member, she must soon become an important
power, and must always be, in many respects,
an uncongenial one. It was best that she
should keep wholly out of European politics,
even of such leagues as one for the suppression of the slave trade. He added, that he did
not wish his language to be construed as im-
porting "an unsocial and sulky spirit on the
part of the United States;" for no such tem-

per existed; it had simply been the policy of
Europe to consider this country as standing
aloof from all European federations, and in this
treatment " we had acquiesced, because it fell
in with our own policy."

In a word, Mr. Adams, by his language and
actions, established and developed precisely that
doctrine which has since been adopted by this
country under the doubly incorrect name of the
" Monroe Doctrine," — a name doubly incorrect, because even the real " Monroe Doctrine "
was not an original idea of Mr. Monroe, and
because the doctrine which now goes by that
name is not identical with the doctrine which
Monroe did once declare.   Mr. Adams's principle was simply that the United States would
take no part whatsoever in foreign politics, not
even in those of South America, save in the extreme event, eliminated from among things possible in this generation, of such an interference
as was contemplated by the Holy Alliance; and
that, on the other hand, she would permit no
European power to gain any new foothold upon
this continent.   Time and experience have not
enabled us to improve upon the principles
which Mr. Adams worked out for us.

Mr. Adams had some pretty stormy times with
Mr. Stratford Canning — the same gentleman
who in his later life is familiar to the readers

of Kinglake's "History of the Crimean War"
as Lord Stratford de Redclyffe, or Eltchi. That
minister's overbearing and dictatorial deportment was afterwards not out of place when he
was representing the protecting power of Great
Britain in the court of the "sick man." But
when he began to display his arrogance in the
face of Mr. Adams he found that he was beard-
ing one who was at least his equal in pride and
temper. The naïve surprise which he manifested on making this discovery is very amusing, and the accounts of the interviews between
the two are among the most pleasing episodes in
the history of our foreign relations. Nor are
they less interesting as a sort of confidential
peep at the asperities of diplomacy. It appears
that besides the composed and formal dignity of
phrase which alone the public knows in published state papers and official correspondence,
there is also an official language of wrath and
retort not at all artificial or stilted, but quite
homelike and human in its sound.

One subject much discussed between Mr.
Adams and Mr. Canning related to the English propositions for joint efforts to suppress
the slave trade. Great Britain had engaged
with much vigor and certainly with an admirable humanity in this cause. Her scheme was
that each power should keep armed cruisers on

the coast of Africa, that the war-ships of either
nation might search the merchant vessels of the
other, and that mixed courts of joint commissioners should try all cases of capture. This
plan had been urged upon the several European nations, but with imperfect success. Portugal, Spain, and the Netherlands had assented
to it; Russia, France, Austria, and Prussia
had rejected it. Mr. Adams's notion was that
the ministry were, in their secret hearts, rather
lukewarm in the business, but that they were
so pressed by "the party of the saints in Parliament" that they were obliged to make a
parade of zeal. Whether this suspicion was
correct or not, it is certain that Mr. Stratford
Canning was very persistent in the presentation of his demands, and could not be persuaded
to take No for an answer. Had it been possible to give any more favorable reply no one
in the United States in that day would have
been better pleased than Mr. Adams to do so.
But the obstacles were insuperable. Besides
the undesirability of departing from the "ex-
tra-European policy," the mixed courts would
have been unconstitutional, and could not have
been established even by act of Congress,
while the claims advanced by Great Britain to
search our ships for English-born seamen in
time of war utterly precluded the possibility

of admitting any rights of search whatsoever
upon her part, even in time of peace, for any
purpose or in any shape. In vain did the Englishman reiterate his appeal. Mr. Adams as
often explained that the insistence of England
upon her outrageous claim had rendered the
United States so sensitive upon the entire subject of search that no description of right of
that kind could ever be tolerated. " All concession of principle," he said, " tended to en-
courage encroachment, and if naval officers
were once habituated to search the vessels of
other nations in time of peace for one thing,
they would be still more encouraged to practise
it for another thing in time of war." The only
way for Great Britain to achieve her purpose
would be " to bind herself by an article, as
strong and explicit as language can make it,
never again in time of war to take a man from
an American vessel." This of course was an
inadmissible proposition, and so Mr. Stratford
Canning's incessant urgency produced no substantial results. This discussion, however, was
generally harmonious. Once only, in its earlier
stages, Mr. Adams notes a remark of Mr. Canning, repeated for the second time, and not altogether gratifying. He said, writes Mr. Adams,
" that he should always receive any observations that I may make to him with a just defer-

ence to my advance of years — over him.   This
is one of those equivocal compliments which,
according to Sterne, a Frenchman always returns with a bow."

It was when they got upon the matter of the
American settlement at the mouth of the Columbia River, that the two struck fire.   Possession of this disputed spot had been taken by the
Americans, but was broken up by the British
during the war of 1812.   After the declaration
of peace upon the *status ante bellum*, a British
government vessel had been dispatched upon the
special errand of making formal return of the
port to the Americans.   In January, 1821,
certain remarks made in debate in the House
of Representatives, followed soon afterward by
publication in the "National Intelligencer" of a
paper signed by Senator Eaton, led Mr. Canning
to think that the Government entertained the
design of establishing a substantial settlement at
the mouth of the river.   On January 26 he called
upon Mr. Adams and inquired the intentions of
the Administration in regard to this.   Mr. Adams
replied that an increase of the present settlement
was not improbable.   Thereupon Mr. Canning
dropping the air of " easy familiarity " which
had previously marked the intercourse between
the two, and " assuming a tone more peremptory "
than Mr. Adams " was disposed to endure," ex-

pressed his great surprise. Mr. Adams "with
a corresponding change of tone" expressed
equal surprise, "both at the form and substance
of his address." Mr. Canning said that "he
conceived such a settlement would be a direct
violation of the article of the Convention of
20th October, 1818." Mr. Adams took down a
volume, read the article, and said, "Now, sir,
if you have any charge to make against the
American Government for a violation of this
article, you will please to make the communication in writing." Mr. Canning retorted, with
great vehemence : —

"'And do you suppose, sir, that I am to be dictated
to as to the manner in which I may think proper to
communicate with the American Government?' I
answered, 'No, sir. We know very well what are the
privileges of foreign ministers, and mean to respect
them. But you will give us leave to determine what
communications we will receive, and how we will receive them; and you may be assured we are as little
disposed to submit to dictation as to exercise it.' He
then, in a louder and more passionate tone of voice,
said : 'And am I to understand that I am to be refused henceforth any conference with you upon the
subject of my mission?' 'Not at all, sir,' said I,
'my request is, that if you have anything further to
say to me *upon this subject*, you would say it in writing. And my motive is to avoid what, both from the
nature of the subject and from the manner in which

you have thought proper to open it, I foresee will tend only to mutual irritation, and not to an amicable arrangement.' With some abatement of tone, but in the same peremptory manner, he said, ' Am I to understand that you refuse any further conference with me on this subject?' I said, ' No. But you will understand that I am not pleased either with the grounds upon which you have sought this conference, nor with the questions which you have seen fit to put to me.' "

Mr. Adams then proceeded to expose the impropriety of a foreign minister demanding from the Administration an explanation of words uttered in debate in Congress, and also said that he supposed that the British had no claim to the territory in question. Mr. Canning rejoined, and referred to the sending out of the American ship of war Ontario, in 1817, without any notice to the British minister [1] at Washington, —

"speaking in a very emphatic manner and as if there had been an intended secret expedition . . . which had been detected only by the vigilance and penetration of the British minister. I answered, ' Why, Mr. Bagot did say something to me about it; but I certainly did not think him serious, and we had a good-humored laughing conversation on the occasion.' Canning, with great vehemence: ' You may rely upon it, sir, that it was no laughing matter to him; for I have seen his report to his government

[1] Then Mr. Bagot.

and know what his feelings concerning it were.' I
replied, 'This is the first intimation I have ever received that Mr. Bagot took the slightest offence at
what then passed between us, . . . and you will give
me leave to say that when he left this country' —
Here I was going to add that the last words he said
to me were words of thanks for the invariable urban-
ity and liberality of my conduct and the personal kindness which he had uniformly received from me. But
I could not finish the sentence. Mr. Canning, in a
paroxysm of extreme irritation, broke out : ' I stop you
there. I will not endure a misrepresentation of what
I say. I never said that Mr. Bagot took offence at
anything that had passed between him and you ; and
nothing that I said imported any such thing.' Then
. . . added in the same passionate manner : ' I am
treated like a school-boy.' I then resumed : ' Mr.
Canning, I have a distinct recollection of the substance of the short conversation between Mr. Bagot
and me at that time ; and it was this ' — ' No doubt,
sir,' said Canning, interrupting me again, ' no doubt,
sir, Mr. Bagot answered you like a man of good
breeding and good humor.' "

Mr. Adams began again and succeeded in
making, without further interruption, a careful
recital of his talk with Mr. Bagot. While he
was speaking Mr. Canning grew cooler, and expressed some surprise at what he heard. But in
a few moments the conversation again became
warm and personal. Mr. Adams remarked that

heretofore he had thrown off some of the "cautious reserve" which might have been "strictly regular" between them, and that

"'so long as his (Canning's) professions had been supported by his conduct'— Here Mr. Canning again stopped me by repeating with great vehemence, 'My conduct! I am responsible for my conduct only to my government!'"

Mr. Adams replied, substantially, that he could respect the rights of Mr. Canning and maintain his own, and that he thought the best mode of treating this topic in future would be by writing. Mr. Canning then expressed himself as

"'willing to forget all that had now passed.' I told him that I neither asked nor promised him to forget. . . . He asked again if he was to understand me as refusing to confer with him further on the subject. I said, 'No.' 'Would I appoint a time for that purpose?' I said, 'Now, if he pleased. . . . But as he appeared to be under some excitement, perhaps he might prefer some other time, in which case I would readily receive him to-morrow at one o'clock;' upon which he rose and took leave, saying he would come at that time."

The next day, accordingly, this genial pair again encountered. Mr. Adams noted at first in Mr. Canning's manner "an effort at coolness,

but no appearance of cheerfulness or good
humor. I saw there was no relaxation of the
tone he had yesterday assumed, and felt that
none would on my part be suitable." They
went over quietly enough some of the ground
traversed the day before, Mr. Adams again ex-
plaining the impropriety of Mr. Canning ques-
tioning him concerning remarks made in debate
in Congress. It was, he said, as if Mr. Rush,
hearing in the House of Commons something
said about sending troops to the Shetland Islands, should proceed to question Lord Castlereagh about it.

" ' Have you,' said Mr. Canning, 'any claim to the
Shetland Islands?' 'Have you any *claim*,' said I,
'to the mouth of Columbia River?' 'Why, do you
not *know*,' replied he, 'that we have a claim?' 'I do
not *know*,' said I, 'what you claim nor what you do
not claim. You claim India; you claim Africa; you
claim' — 'Perhaps,' said he, 'a piece of the moon.'
'No,' said I, 'I have not heard that you claim exclusively any part of the moon; but there is not a spot
on *this* habitable globe that I could affirm you do not
claim!'"

The conversation continued with alternations of
lull and storm, Mr. Canning at times becoming
warm and incensed and interrupting Mr. Adams,
who retorted with a dogged asperity which must
have been extremely irritating. Mr. Adams

said that he did "not expect to be plied with
captious questions" to obtain indirectly that
which had been directly denied.   Mr. Canning,
"exceedingly irritated," complained of the word
"captious."   Mr. Adams retaliated by reciting
offensive language used by Mr. Canning, who
in turn replied that he had been speaking only
in self-defence.   Mr. Canning found occasion
to make again his peculiarly rasping remark
that he should always strive to show towards
Mr. Adams the deference due to his "more advanced years."   After another very uncomfortable passage, Mr. Adams said that the behavior
of Mr. Canning in making the observations of
members of Congress a basis of official interro-
gations was a pretension the more necessary to
be resisted because this

"'was not the first time it had been raised by a
British minister here.'   He asked, with great emo-
tion, who that minister was.   I answered, 'Mr. Jackson.'   'And you got rid of him!' said Mr. Canning,
in a tone of violent ·passion — 'and you got rid of
him! — and you got rid of him!'   This repetition of
the same words, always in the same tone, was with
pauses of a few seconds between each of them, as if
for a reply.   I said: 'Sir, my reference to the pretension of Mr. Jackson was not' —   Here Mr.
Canning interrupted me by saying: 'If you think
that by reference to Mr. Jackson I am to be intimi-

dated from the performance of my duty you will find
yourself greatly mistaken.' 'I had not, sir,' said I,
'the most distant intention of intimidating you from
the performance of your duty ; nor was it with the
intention of alluding to any subsequent occurrences
of his mission ; but ' — Mr. Canning interrupted
me again by saying, still in a tone of high exasperation, — ' Let me tell you, sir, that your reference
to the case of Mr. Jackson is *exceedingly offensive.*'
' I do not know,' said I, ' whether I shall be able to
finish what I intended to say, under such continual
interruptions.' "

Mr. Canning thereupon intimated by a bow his
willingness to listen, and Mr. Adams reiterated
what in a more fragmentary way he had already
said. Mr. Canning then made a formal speech,
mentioning his desire " to cultivate harmony
and smooth down all remnants of asperity between the two countries," again gracefully referred to the deference which he should at all
times pay to Mr. Adams's age, and closed by
declaring, with a significant emphasis, that he
would " never forget the respect due from him
to the American Government." Mr. Adams
bowed in silence and the stormy interview
ended. A day or two afterward the disputants
met by accident, and Mr. Canning showed such
signs of resentment that there passed between
them a " bare salutation."

In the condition of our relations with Great
Britain at the time of these interviews any
needless ill-feeling was strongly to be deprecated.   But Mr. Adams's temperament was
such that he always saw the greater chance of
success in strong and spirited conduct; nor
could he endure that the dignity of the Republic, any more than its safety, should take detriment in his hands.   Moreover he understood
Englishmen better perhaps than they have ever
been understood by any other of the public men
of the United States, and he handled and sub-
dued them with a temper and skill highly agreeable to contemplate.   The President supported
him fully throughout the matter, and the discomfiture and wrath of Mr. Canning never became
even indirectly a cause of regret to the country.

As the years allotted to Monroe passed on,
the manœuvring among the candidates for the
succession to the Presidency grew in activity.
There were several possible presidents in the
field, and during the "era of good feeling"
many an aspiring politician had his brief period
of mild expectancy followed in most cases only
too surely by a hopeless relegation to obscurity.
There were, however, four whose anticipations
rested upon a substantial basis.   William H.
Crawford, Secretary of the Treasury, had been
the rival of Monroe for nomination by the Con-

Stratford de R.

gressional caucus, and had then developed sufficient strength to make him justly sanguine that he might stand next to Monroe in the succession as he apparently did in the esteem of their common party. Mr. Clay, Speaker of the House of Representatives, had such expectations as might fairly grow out of his brilliant reputation, powerful influence in Congress, and great personal popularity. Mr. Adams was pointed out not only by his deserts but also by his position in the Cabinet, it having been the custom heretofore to promote the Secretary of State to the Presidency. It was not until the time of election was near at hand that the strength of General Jackson, founded of course upon the effect of his military prestige upon the masses of the people, began to appear to the other competitors a formidable element in the great rivalry. For a while Mr. Calhoun might have been regarded as a fifth, since he had already become the great chief of the South; but this cause of his strength was likewise his weakness, since it was felt that the North was fairly entitled to present the next candidate. The others, who at one time and another had aspirations, like De Witt Clinton and Tompkins, were never really formidable, and may be disregarded as insignificant threads in the complex political snarl which must be unravelled.

As a study of the dark side of political
society during this period Mr. Adams's Diary
is profoundly interesting. He writes with a
charming absence of reserve. If he thinks
there is rascality at work, he sets down the
names of the knaves and expounds their various
villainies of act and motive with delightfully
outspoken frankness. All his life he was somewhat prone, it must be confessed, to depreciate
the moral characters of others, and to suspect
unworthy designs in the methods or ends of those
who crossed his path. It was the not unnatural
result of his own rigid resolve to be honest.
Refraining with the stern conscientiousness,
which was in the composition of his Puritan
blood, from every act, whether in public or in
private life, which seemed to him in the least
degree tinged with immorality, he found a sort
of compensation for the restraints and discom-
forts of his own austerity in judging severely the
less punctilious world around him. Whatever
other faults he had, it is unquestionable that
his uprightness was as consistent and unvarying
as can be reached by human nature. Yet his
temptations were made the greater and the
more cruel by the beliefs constantly borne in
upon him that his rivals did not accept for their
own governance in the contest the same rules
by which he was pledged to himself to abide.

Jealousy enhanced suspicion, and suspicion in turn pricked jealousy. It is necessary, therefore, to be somewhat upon our guard in accepting his estimates of men and acts at this period ; though the broad general impression to be gathered from his treatment of his rivals, even in these confidential pages, is favorable at least to his justice of disposition and honesty of intention.

At the outset Mr. Clay excited Mr. Adams's most lively resentment. The policy which seemed most promising to that gentleman lay in antagonism to the Administration, whereas, in the absence of substantial party issues, there seemed, at least to members of that Administration, to be no proper grounds for such antagonism. When, therefore, Mr. Clay found or devised such grounds, the President and his Cabinet, vexed and harassed by the opposition of so influential a man, not unnaturally attributed his tactics to selfish and, in a political sense, corrupt motives. Thus Mr. Adams stigmatized his opposition to the Florida treaty as prompted by no just objection to its stipulations, but by a malicious wish to bring discredit upon the negotiator. Probably the charge was true, and Mr. Clay's honesty in opposing an admirable treaty can only be vindicated at the expense of his understanding, — an explanation certainly not to be accepted. But when Mr. Adams attributed to the same motive of embarrassing the Administration Mr. Clay's energetic endeavors to force a recognition of the insurgent states of South America, he exaggerated the inimical element in his rival's motives. It was the business of the President and Cabinet, and preëminently of the Secretary of State, to see to it that the country should not move too fast in this very nice and perilous matter of recognizing the independence of rebels. Mr. Adams was the responsible minister, and had to hold the reins; Mr. Clay, outside the official vehicle, cracked the lash probably a little more loudly than he would have done had he been on the coach-box. It may be assumed that in advocating his various motions looking to the appointment of ministers to the new states and to other acts of recognition, he felt his eloquence rather fired than dampened by the thought of how much trouble he was making for Mr. Adams; but that he was at the same time espousing the cause to which he sincerely wished well is probably true. His ardent temper was stirred by this struggle for independence, and his rhetorical nature could not resist the opportunities for fervid and brilliant oratory presented by this struggle for freedom against mediæval despotism. Real convictions were sometimes diluted with rodomontade, and a true feeling was to some extent stimulated by the desire to embarrass a rival.

Entire freedom from prejudice would have
been too much to expect from Mr. Adams; but
his criticisms of Clay are seldom marked by any
serious accusations or really bitter explosions of
ill-temper.   Early in his term of office he writes
that Mr. Clay has "already mounted his South
American great horse," and that his "project
is that in which John Randolph failed, to control or overthrow the Executive by swaying the
House of Representatives."   Again he says that
"Clay is as rancorously benevolent as John
Randolph."   The sting of these remarks lay
rather in the comparison with Randolph than
in their direct allegations.   In January, 1819,
Adams notes that Clay has "redoubled his rancor against me," and gives himself "free swing
to assault me . . . both in his public speeches
and by secret machinations, without scruple or
delicacy."   The diarist gloomily adds, that "all
public business in Congress now connects itself
with intrigues, and there is great danger that
the whole Government will degenerate into a
struggle of cabals."   He was rather inclined to
such pessimistic vaticinations; but it must be
confessed that he spoke with too much reason
on this occasion.   In the absence of a sufficient
supply of important public questions to absorb
the energies of the men in public life, the petty
game of personal politics was playing with un-

usual zeal.   As time went on, however, and the
South American questions were removed from
the arena, Adams's ill-feeling towards Clay became greatly mitigated. Clay's assaults and
opposition also gradually dwindled away; go-
betweens carried to and fro disclaimers, made
by the principals, of personal ill-will towards
each other; and before the time of election was
actually imminent something as near the *en-
tente cordiale* was established as could be reasonably expected to exist between competitors
very unlike both in moral and mental constitution.[1]

Mr. Adams's unbounded indignation and profound contempt were reserved for Mr. Crawford,
partly, it may be suspected by the cynically
minded, because Crawford for a long time seemed
to be by far the most formidable rival, but
partly also because Crawford was in fact unable to resist the temptation to use ignoble
means for attaining an end which he coveted
too keenly for his own honor.   It was only by
degrees that Adams began to suspect the under-
hand methods and malicious practices of Crawford; but as conviction was gradually brought
home to him his native tendency towards suspicion was enhanced to an extreme degree.   He

[1] For a deliberate estimate of Clay's character see Mr.
Adams's Diary, v. 325.

then came to recognize in Crawford a wholly
selfish and scheming politician, who had the
baseness to retain his seat in Mr. Monroe's Cabinet with the secret persistent object of giving
the most fatal advice in his power. From that
time forth he saw in every suggestion made by
the Secretary of the Treasury only an insidious
intent to lead the Administration, and especially
the Department of State, into difficulty, failure,
and disrepute. He notes, evidently with perfect belief, that for this purpose Crawford was
even covertly busy with the Spanish ambassador
to prevent an accommodation of our differences
with Spain. "Oh, the windings of the human
heart!" he exclaims; "possibly Crawford is not
himself conscious of his real motives for this
conduct." Even the slender measure of charity
involved in this last sentence rapidly evaporated
from the poisoned atmosphere of his mind. He
mentions that Crawford has killed a man in a
duel; that he leaves unanswered a pamphlet
" supported by documents " exhibiting him " in
the most odious light, as sacrificing every principle to his ambition." Because Calhoun would
not support him for the Presidency, Crawford
stimulated a series of attacks upon the War Department. He was the " instigator and animat-
ing spirit of the whole movement both in Congress and at Richmond against Jackson and the

Administration." He was " a worm preying
upon the vitals of the Administration in its own
body." He "solemnly deposed in a court of
justice that which is not true," for the purpose
of bringing discredit upon the testimony given
by Mr. Adams in the same cause. But Mr.
Adams says of this that he cannot bring himself to believe that Crawford has been guilty of
wilful falsehood, though convicted of inaccuracy
by his own words; for " ambition debauches
memory itself." A little later he would have
been less merciful. In some vexatious and difficult commercial negotiations which Mr. Adams
was conducting with France, Crawford is "afraid
of [the result] being too favorable."

To form a just opinion of the man thus un-
pleasantly sketched is difficult. For nearly eight
years Mr. Adams was brought into close and
constant relations with him, and as a result
formed a very low opinion of his character and
by no means a high estimate of his abilities.
Even after making a liberal allowance for
the prejudice naturally supervening from their
rivalry there is left a residuum of condemnation
abundantly sufficient to ruin a more vigorous
reputation than Crawford has left behind him.
Apparently Mr. Calhoun, though a fellow
Southerner, thought no better of the ambitious
Georgian than did Mr. Adams, to whom one

day he remarked that Crawford was "a very singular instance of a man of such character rising to the eminence he now occupies; that there has not been in the history of the Union another man with abilities so ordinary, with services so slender, and so thoroughly corrupt, who had contrived to make himself a candidate for the Presidency." Nor was this a solitary expression of the feelings of the distinguished South Carolinian.

Mr. E. H. Mills, Senator from Massachusetts, and a dispassionate observer, speaks of Crawford with scant favor as "coarse, rough, uneducated, of a pretty strong mind, a great intriguer, and determined to make himself President." He adds: "Adams, Jackson, and Calhoun all think well of each other, and are united at least in one thing, — to wit, a most thorough dread and abhorrence of Crawford."

Yet Crawford was for many years not only never without eager expectations of his own, which narrowly missed realization and might not have missed it had not his health broken down a few months too soon, but he had a large following, strong friends, and an extensive influence. But if he really had great ability he had not the good fortune of an opportunity to show it; and he lives in history rather as a man from whom much was expected than as a man who achieved much. One faculty, however, not of the best, but serviceable, he had in a rare degree : he thoroughly understood all the artifices of politics ; he knew how to interest and organize partisans, to obtain newspaper support, and generally to extend and direct his following after that fashion which soon afterward began to be fully developed by the younger school of our public men. He was the *avant courier* of a bad system, of which the first crude manifestations were received with well-merited disrelish by the worthier among his contemporaries.

It is the more easy to believe that Adams's distrust of Crawford was a sincere conviction, when we consider his behavior towards another dangerous rival, General Jackson. In view of the new phase which the relationship between these two men was soon to take on, Adams's hearty championship of Jackson for several years prior to 1825 deserves mention. The Secretary stood gallantly by the General at a crisis in Jackson's life when he greatly needed such strong official backing, and in an hour of extreme need Adams alone in the Cabinet of Monroe lent an assistance which Jackson afterwards too readily forgot. Seldom has a government been brought by the undue zeal of its servants into a quandary more perplexing than that into which the reckless military hero brought the

Administration of President Monroe. Turned
loose in the regions of Florida, checked only by
an uncertain and disputed boundary line running
through half-explored forests, confronted by a
hated foe whose strength he could well afford
to despise, General Jackson, in a war properly
waged only against Indians, ran a wild and
lawless, but very vigorous and effective, career
in Spanish possessions. He hung a couple of
British subjects with as scant trial and meagre
shrift as if he had been a mediæval free-lance ;
he marched upon Spanish towns and peremp-
torily forced the blue-blooded commanders to
capitulate in the most humiliating manner ;
afterwards, when the Spanish territory had become American, in his civil capacity as Governor, he flung the Spanish Commissioner into
jail. He treated instructions, laws, and established usages as teasing cobwebs which any
spirited public servant was in duty bound to
break ; then he quietly stated his willingness to
let the country take the benefit of his irregular
proceedings and make him the scapegoat or
martyr if such should be needed. How to treat
this too successful chieftain was no simple problem. He had done what he ought not to have
done, yet everybody in the country was heartily
glad that he had done it. He ought not to have
hung Arbuthnot and Ambrister, nor to have

seized Pensacola, nor later on to have imprisoned
Callava; yet the general efficiency of his pro-
cedure fully accorded with the secret disposition
of the country. It was, however, not easy to
establish the propriety of his trenchant doings
upon any acknowledged principles of law, and
during the long period through which these dis-
turbing feats extended, Jackson was left in
painful solitude by those who felt obliged to
judge his actions by rule rather than by sympathy. The President was concerned lest his
Administration should be brought into indefen-
sible embarrassment; Calhoun was personally
displeased because the instructions issued from
his department had been exceeded; Crawford
eagerly sought to make the most of such admirable opportunities for destroying the prestige
of one who might grow into a dangerous rival;
Clay, who hated a military hero, indulged in a
series of fierce denunciations in the House of
Representatives; Mr. Adams alone stood gallantly by the man who had dared to take vigorous measures upon his own sole responsibility.
His career touched a kindred chord in Adams's
own independent and courageous character, and
perhaps for the only time in his life the Secretary of State became almost sophistical in the
arguments by which he endeavored to sustain
the impetuous warrior against an adverse Cab-

inet. The authority given to Jackson to cross
the Spanish frontier in pursuit of the Indian
enemy was justified as being only defensive warfare ; then " all the rest," argued Adams, " even
to the order for taking the Fort of Barrancas by
storm, was incidental, deriving its character from
the object, which was not hostility to Spain, but
the termination of the Indian war." Through
long and anxious sessions Adams stood fast in
opposing " the unanimous opinions " of the
President, Crawford, Calhoun, and Wirt. Their
policy seemed to him a little ignoble and wholly
blundering, because, he said, " it is weakness
and a confession of weakness. The disclaimer
of power in the Executive is of dangerous example and of evil consequences. There is injustice to the officer in disavowing him, when in
principle he is strictly justifiable." This behavior upon Mr. Adams's part was the more
generous and disinterested because the earlier
among these doings of Jackson incensed Don
Onis extremely and were near bringing about
the entire disruption of that important negotiation with Spain upon which Mr. Adams had so
much at stake. But few civilians have had a
stronger dash of the fighting element than had
Mr. Adams, and this impelled him irresistibly
to stand shoulder to shoulder with Jackson in
such an emergency, regardless of possible con-

sequences to himself. He preferred to insist
that the hanging of Arbuthnot and Ambrister
was according to the laws of war and to maintain that position in the teeth of Stratford
Canning rather than to disavow it and render
apology and reparation. So three years later
when Jackson was again in trouble by reason of
his arrest of Callava, he still found a stanch
advocate in Adams, who, having made an argument for the defence which would have done
credit to a subtle-minded barrister, concluded
by adopting the sentiment of Hume concerning
the execution of Don Pantaleon de Sa by Oliver
Cromwell, — if the laws of nations had been
violated, "it was by a signal act of justice deserving universal approbation."   Later still, on
January 8, 1824, being the anniversary of the
victory of New Orleans, as if to make a conspicuous declaration of his opinions in favor of
Jackson, Mr. Adams gave a great ball in his
honor, "at which about one thousand persons
attended." [1]

[1] Senator Mills says of this grand ball: "Eight large
rooms were open and literally filled to overflowing. There
must have been at least a thousand people there ; and so far
as Mr. Adams was concerned it certainly evinced a great deal
of taste, elegance, and good sense. . . . Many stayed till
twelve and one. . . . It is the universal opinion that nothing
has ever equalled this party here either in brilliancy of preparation or elegance of the company."

He was in favor of offering to the General
the position of minister to Mexico ; and before
Jackson had developed into a rival of himself
for the Presidency, he exerted himself to secure
the Vice-Presidency for him.   Thus by argument and by influence in the Cabinet, in many
a private interview, and in the world of society,
also by wise counsel when occasion offered, Mr.
Adams for many years made himself the note-
worthy and indeed the only powerful friend of
General Jackson.   Nor up to the last moment,
and when Jackson had become his most dangerous competitor, is there any derogatory passage
concerning him in the Diary.

As the period of election drew nigh, interest
in it absorbed everything else ; indeed during
the last year of Monroe's Administration public
affairs were so quiescent and the public business
so seldom transcended the simplest routine, that
there was little else than the next Presidency to
be thought or talked of.   The rivalship for this,
as has been said, was based not upon conflicting
theories concerning public affairs, but solely
upon individual preference for one or another
of four men no one of whom at that moment
represented any great principle in antagonism
to any of the others.   Under no circumstances
could the temptation to petty intrigue and malicious tale-bearing be greater than when votes

were to be gained or lost solely by personal pre-
dilection. In such a contest Adams was severely
handicapped as against the showy prestige of
the victorious soldier, the popularity of the
brilliant orator, and the artfulness of the most
dexterous political manager then in public life.
Long prior to this stage Adams had established
his rule of conduct in the campaign. So early as
March, 1818, he was asked one day by Mr. Everett whether he was "determined to do nothing
with a view to promote his future election to the
Presidency as the successor of Mr. Monroe,"
and he had replied that he "should do absolutely nothing." To this resolution he sturdily
adhered. Not a breach of it was ever brought
home to him, or indeed — save in one instance
soon to be noticed — seriously charged against
him. There is not in the Diary the faintest
trace of any act which might be so much as
questionable or susceptible of defence only by
casuistry. That he should have perpetuated
evidence of any flagrant misdoing certainly
could not be expected; but in a record kept
with the fulness and frankness of this Diary we
should read between the lines and detect as it
were in its general flavor any taint of disingen-
uousness or concealment; we should discern
moral unwholesomeness in its atmosphere. A
thoughtless sentence would slip from the pen,

a sophistical argument would be formulated
for self-comfort, some acquaintance, interview,
or arrangement would slide upon some un-
guarded page indicative of undisclosed matters.
But there is absolutely nothing of this sort.
There is no tinge of bad color; all is clear as
crystal. Not an editor, nor a member of Congress, nor a local politician, not even a private
individual, was intimidated or conciliated. On
the contrary it often happened that those who
made advances, at least sometimes stimulated
by honest friendship, got rebuffs instead of
encouragement. Even after the contest was
known to have been transferred to the House
of Representatives, when Washington was actually buzzing with the ceaseless whisperings of
many secret conclaves, when the air was thick
with rumors of what this one had said and that
one had done, when, as Webster said, there
were those who pretended to foretell how a representative would vote from the way in which
he put on his hat, when of course stories of
intrigue and corruption poisoned the honest
breeze, and when the streets seemed traversed
only by the busy tread of the go-betweens, the
influential friends, the wire-pullers of the various contestants, — still amid all this noisy excitement and extreme temptation Mr. Adams
held himself almost wholly aloof, wrapped in the

cloak of his rigid integrity. His proud honesty
was only not quite repellent; he sometimes allowed himself to answer questions courteously,
and for a brief period held in check his strong
natural propensity to give offence and make enemies. This was the uttermost length that he
could go towards political corruption. He became for a few weeks tolerably civil of speech,
which after all was much for him to do and
doubtless cost him no insignificant effort. Since
the days of Washington he alone presents the
singular spectacle of a candidate for the Presidency deliberately taking the position, and in
a long campaign really never flinching from it :
" that, if the people wish me to be President I
shall not refuse the office ; but I ask nothing
from any man or from any body of men."

Yet though he declined to be a courtier of
popular favor he did not conceal from himself
or from others the chagrin which he would feel
if there should be a manifestation of popular
disfavor. Before the popular election he stated
that if it should go against him he should con-
strue it as the verdict of the people that they
were dissatisfied with his services as a public
man, and he should then retire to private life,
no longer expecting or accepting public functions. He did not regard politics as a struggle

in which, if he should now be beaten in one encounter, he would return to another in the hope
of better success in time. His notion was that
the people had had ample opportunity during
his incumbency in appointive offices to measure
his ability and understand his character, and
that the action of the people in electing or not
electing him to the Presidency would be an indication that they were satisfied or dissatisfied
with him. In the latter event he had nothing
more to seek. Politics did not constitute a profession or career in which he felt entitled to
persist in seeking personal success as he might
in the law or in business. Neither did the circumstances of the time place him in the position
of an advocate of any great principle which he
might feel it his duty to represent and to fight
for against any number of reverses. No such
element was present at this time in national affairs. He construed the question before the
people simply as concerning their opinion of
him. He was much too proud to solicit and
much too honest to scheme for a favorable expression. It was a singular and a lofty attitude
even if a trifle egotistical and not altogether
unimpeachable by argument. It could not di-
minish but rather it intensified his interest in a
contest which he chose to regard not simply as

a struggle for a glittering prize but as a judgment upon the services which he had been for a lifetime rendering to his countrymen.

How profoundly his whole nature was moved by the position in which he stood is evident, often almost painfully, in the Diary. Any attempt to conceal his feeling would be idle, and he makes no such attempt. He repeats all the rumors which come to his ears; he tells the stories about Crawford's illness; he records his own temptations; he tries hard to nerve himself to bear defeat philosophically by constantly predicting it; indeed, he photographs his whole existence for many weeks; and however eagerly any person may aspire to the Presidency of the United States there is little in the picture to make one long for the preliminary position of candidate for that honor. It is too much like the stake and the flames through which the martyr passed to eternal beatitude, with the difference as against the candidate that he has by no means the martyr's certainty of reward.

In those days of slow communication it was not until December, 1824, that it became everywhere known that there had been no election of a president by the people. When the Electoral College met the result of their ballots was as follows: —

General Jackson led with . . 99 votes.
Adams followed with . . . . 84 "
Crawford had . . . . . . 41 "
Clay had . . . . 37 "

Total . . . . 261 votes.

Mr. Calhoun was elected Vice-President by
the handsome number of 182 votes.

This condition of the election had been quite
generally anticipated; yet Mr. Adams's friends
were not without some feeling of disappointment. They had expected for him a fair support at the South, whereas he in fact received
seventy-seven out of his eighty-four votes from
New York and New England; Maryland gave
him three, Louisiana gave him two, Delaware
and Illinois gave him one each.

When the electoral body was known to be
reduced within the narrow limits of the House
of Representatives, intrigue was rather stimulated than diminished by the definiteness
which became possible for it. Mr. Clay, who
could not come before the House, found himself transmuted from a candidate to a President-
maker; for it was admitted by all that his great
personal influence in Congress would almost
undoubtedly confer success upon the aspirant
whom he should favor. Apparently his predilections were at least possibly in favor of Craw-

ford ; but Crawford's health had been for many
months very bad ; he had had a severe paralytic
stroke, and when acting as Secretary of the
Treasury he had been unable to sign his name,
so that a stamp or die had been used ; his
speech was scarcely intelligible ; and when Mr.
Clay visited him in the retirement in which his
friends now kept him, the fact could not be
concealed that he was for the time at least a
wreck.   Mr. Clay therefore had to decide for
himself, his followers, and the country whether
Mr. Adams or General Jackson should be the
next President of the United States.   A cruel
attempt was made in this crisis either to destroy
his influence by blackening his character, or to
intimidate him, through fear of losing his reputation for integrity, into voting for Jackson.
An anonymous letter charged that the friends
of Clay had hinted that, "like the Swiss, they
would fight for those who pay best;" that they
had offered to elect Jackson if he would agree
to make Clay Secretary of State, and that upon
his indignant refusal to make such a bargain
the same proposition had been made to Mr.
Adams, who was found less scrupulous and had
promptly formed the "unholy coalition."   This
wretched publication, made a few days before
the election in the House, was traced to a
dull-witted Pennsylvania Representative by the

name of Kremer, who had obviously been used as a tool by cleverer men. It met, however, the fate which seems happily always to attend such ignoble devices, and failed utterly of any more important effect than the utter annihilation of Kremer. In truth, General Jackson's fate had been sealed from the instant when it had fallen into Mr. Clay's hands. Clay had long since expressed his unfavorable opinion of the "military hero," in terms too decisive to admit of explanation or retraction. Without much real liking for Adams, Clay at least disliked him much less than he did Jackson, and certainly his honest judgment favored the civilian far more than the disorderly soldier whose lawless career in Florida had been the topic of some of the great orator's fiercest invective. The arguments founded on personal fitness were strongly upon the side of Adams, and other arguments advanced by the Jacksonians could hardly deceive Clay. They insisted that their candidate was the choice of the people so far as a superiority of preference had been indicated, and that therefore he ought to be also the choice of the House of Representatives. It would be against the spirit of the Constitution and a thwarting of the popular will, they said, to prefer either of his competitors. The fallacy of this reasoning, if reasoning it could be called, was glaring. If

the spirit of the Constitution required **the**
House of Representatives not to *elect* from
three candidates before it, but only to induct
an individual into the Presidency by a process
which was in form voting but in fact only a
simple certification that he had received the
highest number of electoral votes, it would have
been a plain and easy matter for the letter of
the Constitution to have expressed this spirit, or
indeed to have done away altogether with this
machinery of a sham election. The Jackson
men had only to state their argument in order
to expose its hollowness; for they said substantially that the Constitution established an election without an option; that the electors were
to vote for a person predestined by an earlier
occurrence to receive their ballots. But besides
their unsoundness in argument, their statistical
position was far from being what they under-
took to represent it. The popular vote had
been so light that it really looked as though
the people had cared very little which candidate
should succeed; and to talk about a manifestation of the *popular will* was absurd, for the
only real manifestation had been of popular indifference. For example, in 1823 Massachusetts had cast upwards of 66,000 votes in the
state election, whereas in this national election
she cast only a trifle more than 37,000. Vir-

ginia distributed a total of less than 15,000 among all four candidates.   Pluralities did not signify much in such a condition of sentiment as was indicated by these figures.   Moreover, in six States, viz., Vermont, New York, Delaware, South Carolina, Georgia, Louisiana, the electors were chosen by the legislatures, not by the people ; so that there was no correct way of counting them at all in a discussion of pluralities. Guesses and approximations favored Adams, and to an important degree ; for these six States gave to Adams thirty-six votes, to Jackson nineteen, to Crawford six, to Clay four.   In New York, Jackson had hardly an appreciable following.   Moreover, in other States many thousands of votes which had been "cast for no candidate in particular, but in opposition to the caucus ticket generally," were reckoned as if they had been cast for Jackson or against Adams, as suited the especial case.   Undoubtedly Jackson did have a plurality, but undoubtedly it fell very far short of the imposing figure, nearly 48,000, which his supporters had the audacity to name.

The election took place in the House on February 9, 1825.   Daniel Webster and John Randolph were tellers, and they reported that there were " for John Quincy Adams, of Massachusetts, thirteen votes; for Andrew Jackson, of Tennessee, seven votes; for William H. Crawford, of Georgia, four votes." Thereupon the speaker announced Mr. Adams to have been elected President of the United States.

This end of an unusually exciting contest thus left Mr. Adams in possession of the field, Mr. Crawford the victim of an irretrievable defeat, Mr. Clay still hopeful and aspiring for a future which had only disappointment in store for him, General Jackson enraged and revengeful. Not even Mr. Adams was fully satisfied. When the committee waited upon him to inform him of the election, he referred in his reply to the peculiar state of things and said, "could my refusal to accept the trust thus delegated to me give an opportunity to the people to form and to express with a nearer approach to unanimity the object of their preference, I should not hesitate to decline the acceptance of this eminent charge and to submit the decision of this momentous question again to their decision." That this singular and striking statement was made in good faith is highly probable. William H. Seward says that it was "unquestionably uttered with great sincerity of heart." The test of action of course could not be applied, since the resignation of Mr. Adams would only have made Mr. Calhoun President, and could not have been so arranged as to bring about a new election. Otherwise the course of

his argument would have been clear; the fact
that such action involved an enormous sacrifice
would have been to his mind strong evidence
that it was a duty; and the temptation to perform a duty, always strong with him, became
ungovernable if the duty was exceptionally disagreeable.   Under the circumstances, however,
the only logical conclusion lay in the inauguration, which took place in the customary simple
fashion on March 4, 1825.   Mr. Adams, we are
told, was dressed in a black suit, of which all
the materials were wholly of American man-
ufacture.   Prominent among those who after
the ceremony hastened to greet him and to
shake hands with him appeared General Jackson.   It was the last time that any friendly
courtesy is recorded as having passed between
the two.

Many men eminent in public affairs have had
their best years embittered by their failure to
secure the glittering prize of the Presidency.
Mr. Adams is perhaps the only person to whom
the gaining of that proud distinction has been
in some measure a cause of chagrin.   This
strange sentiment, which he undoubtedly felt,
was due to the fact that what he had wished
was not the office in and for itself, but the office
as a symbol or token of the popular approval.
He had held important and responsible public

positions during substantially his whole active
life; he was nearly sixty years old, and, as he
said, he now for the first time had an opportunity to find out in what esteem the people of
the country held him. What he wished was
that the people should now express their decided
satisfaction with him. This he hardly could be
said to have obtained; though to be the choice
of a plurality in the nation and then to be selected by so intelligent a body of constituents
as the Representatives of the United States
involved a peculiar sanction, yet nothing else
could fully take the place of that national in-
dorsement which he had coveted. When men
publicly profess modest depreciation of their
successes they are seldom believed; but in his
private Diary Mr. Adams wrote, on December
31, 1825: —

"The year has been the most momentous of those
that have passed over my head, inasmuch as it has
witnessed my elevation at the age of fifty-eight to the
Chief Magistracy of my country, to the summit of
laudable or at least blameless worldly ambition; not
however in a manner satisfactory to pride or to just
desire; not by the unequivocal suffrages of a majority
of the people; with perhaps two thirds of the whole
people adverse to the actual result."

No President since Washington had ever
come into office so entirely free from any man-

ner of personal obligations or partisan entanglements, express or implied, as did Mr. Adams.
Throughout the campaign he had not himself,
or by any agent, held out any manner of tacit
inducement to any person whomsoever, con-
tingent upon his election. He entered upon
the Presidency under no indebtedness. He at
once nominated his Cabinet as follows: Henry
Clay, Secretary of State; Richard Rush, Secretary of the Treasury; James Barbour, Secretary of War; Samuel L. Southard, Secretary
of the Navy; William Wirt, Attorney-General.
The last two were renominations of the incumbents under Monroe. The entire absence of
chicanery or the use of influence in the distribution of offices is well illustrated by the following incident: On the afternoon following
the day of inauguration President Adams called
upon Rufus King, whose term of service as Senator from New York had just expired, and who
was preparing to leave Washington on the next
day. In the course of a conversation concerning the nominations which had been sent to the
Senate that forenoon the President said that
he had nominated no minister to the English
court, and

"asked Mr. King if he would accept that mission.
His first and immediate impulse was to decline it. He
said that his determination to retire from the public

service had been made up, and that this proposal was utterly unexpected to him. Of this I was aware; but I urged upon him a variety of considerations to induce his acceptance of it. . . . I dwelt with earnestness upon all these motives, and apparently not without effect. He admitted the force of them, and finally promised fully to consider of the proposal before giving me a definite answer."

The result was an acceptance by Mr. King, his nomination by the President, and confirmation by the Senate. He was an old Federalist, to whom Mr. Adams owed no favors. With such directness and simplicity were the affairs of the Republic conducted. It is a quaint and pleasing scene from the period of our forefathers: the President, without discussion of "claims" to a distinguished and favorite post, actually selects for it a member of a hostile political organization, an old man retiring from public life; then quietly walks over to his house, surprises him with the offer, and finding him reluctant urgently presses upon him arguments to induce his acceptance. But the whole business of office-seeking and office-distributing, now so overshadowing, had no place under Mr. Adams. On March 5 he sent in several nominations which were nearly all of previous incumbents. "Efforts had been made," he writes, "by some of the senators to obtain

different nominations, and to introduce a principle of change or rotation in office at the ex-
piration of these commissions, which would
make the Government a perpetual and unin-
termitting scramble for office. A more perni-
cious expedient could scarcely have been devised. . . . I determined to renominate every
person against whom there was no complaint
which would have warranted his removal." A
notable instance was that of Sterret, naval officer
at New Orleans, " a noisy and clamorous reviler
of the Administration," and lately busy in a
project for insulting a Louisiana Representative
who had voted for Mr. Adams. Secretary Clay
was urgent for the removal of this man, plausi-
bly saying that in the cases of persons holding
office at the pleasure of the Administration the
proper course was to avoid on the one hand political persecution, and on the other any appearance of pusillanimity. Mr. Adams replied that
if Sterret had been actually engaged in insulting
a representative for the honest and independent
discharge of duty, he would make the removal
at once. But the design had not been consum-
mated, and an *intention* never carried into effect
would scarcely justify removal.

" Besides [he added], should I remove this man
for this cause it must be upon some fixed principle,
which would apply to others as well as to him. And

where was it possible to draw the line? Of the custom-house officers throughout the Union, four fifths in all probability were opposed to my election. Crawford, Secretary of the Treasury, had distributed these positions among his own supporters. I had been urged very earnestly and from various quarters to sweep away my opponents and provide with their places for my friends. I can justify the refusal to adopt this policy only by the steadiness and consistency of my adhesion to my own. If I depart from this in one instance I shall be called upon by my friends to do the same in many. An invidious and inquisitorial scrutiny into the personal dispositions of public officers will creep through the whole Union, and the most selfish and sordid passions will be kindled into activity to distort the conduct and misrepresent the feelings of men whose places may become the prize of slander upon them."

Mr. Clay was silenced, and Sterret retained his position, constituting thereafter only a somewhat striking instance among many to show that nothing was to be lost by political opposition to Mr. Adams.

It was a cruel and discouraging fatality which brought about that a man so suicidally upright in the matter of patronage should find that the bitterest abuse which was heaped upon him was founded in an allegation of corruption of precisely this nature. When before the election the ignoble George Kremer anonymously charged

that Mr. Clay had sold his friends in the House
of Representatives to Mr. Adams, "as the
planter does his negroes or the farmer his team
and horses;" when Mr. Clay promptly published
the unknown writer as "a base and infamous
calumniator, a dastard and a liar;" when next
Kremer, being unmasked, avowed that he would
make good his charges, but immediately afterward actually refused to appear or testify before
a Committee of the House instructed to inves-
tigate the matter, it was supposed by all reasonable observers that the outrageous accusation
was forever laid at rest. But this was by no
means the case. The author of the slander had
been personally discredited; but the slander
itself had not been destroyed. So shrewdly
had its devisers who saw future usefulness in it
managed the matter, that while Kremer slunk
away into obscurity, the story which he had
told remained an assertion denied, but not disproved, still open to be believed by suspicious
or willing friends. With Adams President and
Clay Secretary of State and General Jackson
nominated, as he quickly was by the Tennessee Legislature, as a candidate for the next
Presidential term, the accusation was too plausible and too tempting to be allowed to fall forever into dusty death; rather it was speedily
exhumed from its shallow burial and galvanized

into new life. The partisans of General Jackson sent it to and fro throughout the land. No denial, no argument, could kill it. It began to gain that sort of half belief which is certain to result from constant repetition ; since many minds are so constituted that truth may be actually, as it were, manufactured for them by ceaseless iteration of statement, the many hearings gaining the character of evidence.

It is long since all students of American history, no matter what are their prejudices, or in whose interest their researches are prosecuted, have branded this accusation as devoid of even the most shadowy basis of probability, and it now gains no more credit than would a story that Adams, Clay, and Jackson had conspired together to get Crawford out of their way by assassination, and that his paralysis was the result of the drugs and potions administered in performance of this foul plot. But for a while the rumor stalked abroad among the people, and many conspicuously bowed down before it because it served their purpose, and too many others also, it must be confessed, did likewise because they were deceived and really believed it. Even the legislature of Tennessee were not ashamed to give formal countenance to a calumny in support of which not a particle of evidence had ever been adduced. In a preamble to certain resolutions passed by this body upon this subject in 1827, it was recited that : " Mr. Adams desired the office of President ; he went into the combination without it, and came out with it.   Mr. Clay desired that of Secretary of State ; he went into the combination without it, and came out with it."   No other charge could have wounded Mr. Adams so keenly ; yet no course was open to him for refuting the slander.   Mr. Clay, beside himself with a just rage, was better able to fight after the fashion of the day — if indeed he could only find somebody to fight.   This he did at last in the person of John Randolph, of Roanoke, who adverted in one of his rambling and vituperative harangues to " the coalition of Blifil and Black George — the combination unheard of till then of the Puritan and the black-leg."   This language led naturally enough to a challenge from Mr. Clay.   The parties met [1] and exchanged shots without result.   The pistols were a second time loaded ; Clay fired ; Randolph fired into the air, walked up to Clay and without a word gave him his hand, which Clay had as it were perforce to take.   There was no injury done save to the skirts of Randolph's long flannel coat which were pierced by one of the bullets.

By way of revenge a duel may be effective if

[1] April 8, 1826.

the wrong man does not happen to get shot;
but as evidence for intelligent men a bloodier
ending than this would have been inconclusive.
It so happened, however, that Jackson, altogether contrary to his own purpose, brought
conclusive aid to President Adams and Secretary Clay. Whether the General ever had any
real faith in the charge can only be surmised.
Not improbably he did, for his mental workings
were so peculiar in their violence and prejudice
that apparently he always sincerely believed all
persons who crossed his path to be knaves and
villains of the blackest dye. But certain it is
that whether he credited the tale or not he soon
began to devote himself with all his wonted
vigor and pertinacity to its wide dissemination.
Whether in so doing he was stupidly believing a
lie, or intentionally spreading a known slander,
is a problem upon which his friends and bio-
graphers have exhausted much ingenuity without reaching any certain result. But sure it is
that early in the year 1827 he was so far carried
beyond the bounds of prudence as to declare
before many persons that he had proof of the
corrupt bargain. The assertion was promptly
sent to the newspapers by a Mr. Carter Beverly, one of those who heard it made in the
presence of several guests at the Hermitage.
The name of Mr. Beverly, at first concealed,

soon became known, and he was of course compelled to vouch in his principal. General Jackson never deserted his adherents, whether their difficulties were noble or ignoble. He came gallantly to the aid of Mr. Beverly, and in a letter of June 6 declared that early in January, 1825, he had been visited by a " member of Congress of high respectability," who had told him of " a great intrigue going on " of which he ought to be informed. This gentleman had then proceeded to explain that Mr. Clay's friends were afraid that if General Jackson should be elected President, " Mr. Adams would be continued Secretary of State (innuendo, there would be no room for Kentucky) ; that if I would say, or permit any of my confidential friends to say, that in case I were elected President, Mr. Adams should not be continued Secretary of State, by a complete union of Mr. Clay and his friends they would put an end to the Presidential contest in one hour. And he was of opinion it was right to fight such intriguers with their own weapons." This scarcely disguised suggestion of bargain and corruption the General said that he repudiated indignantly. Clay at once publicly challenged Jackson to produce some evidence — to name the " respectable " member of Congress who appeared in the very unrespectable light of advising a candidate for the Presidency to emulate the alleged baseness of his opponents. Jackson thereupon uncovered James Buchanan, of Pennsylvania. Mr. Buchanan was a friend of the General, and to what point it may have been expected or hoped that his allegiance would carry him in support of his chief in this dire hour of extremity is matter only of inference. Fortunately, however, his fealty does not appear to have led him any great distance from the truth. He yielded to the prevailing desire to pass along the responsibility to some one else so far as to try to bring in a Mr. Markley, who, however, never became more than a dumb figure in the drama in which Buchanan was obliged to remain as the last important character. With obvious reluctance this gentleman then wrote that if General Jackson had placed any such construction as the foregoing upon an interview which had occurred between them, and which he recited at length, then the General had totally misconstrued — as was evident enough — what he, Mr. Buchanan, had said. Indeed, that Jackson could have supposed him to entertain the sentiments imputed to him made Mr. Buchanan, as he said, " exceedingly unhappy." In other words, there was no foundation whatsoever for the charge thus traced back to an originator who denied having

originated it and said that it was all a mistake.
General Jackson was left to be defended from
the accusation of deliberate falsehood only by
the charitable suggestion that he had been unable to understand a perfectly simple conversation. Apparently Mr. Adams and Mr. Clay
ought now to be abundantly satisfied, since not
only were they amply vindicated, but their chief
vilifier seemed to have been pierced by the
point which he had sharpened for them. They
had yet, however, to learn what vitality there is
in falsehood.

General Jackson and his friends had alone
played any active part in this matter. Of these
friends Mr. Kremer had written a letter of retraction and apology which he was with difficulty prevented from publishing ; Mr. Buchanan
had denied all that he had been summoned to
prove ; a few years later Mr. Beverly wrote and
sent to Mr. Clay a contrite letter of regret.
General Jackson alone remained for the rest
of his life unsilenced, obstinately reiterating a
charge disproved by his own witnesses. But
worse than all this, accumulations of evidence
long and laboriously sought in many quarters
have established a tolerably strong probability
that advances of precisely the character alleged
against Mr. Adams's friends were made to Mr.
Clay by the most intimate personal associates

of General Jackson. The discussion of this
unpleasant suspicion would not, however, be an
excusable episode in this short volume. The
reader who is curious to pursue the matter further will find all the documentary evidence col-
lected in its original shape in the first volume
of Colton's "Life of Clay," accompanied by an
argument needlessly elaborate and surcharged
with feeling yet in the main sufficiently fair
and exhaustive.

Mr. Benton says that "no President could
have commenced his administration under more
unfavorable auspices, or with less expectation
of a popular career," than did Mr. Adams.
From the first a strong minority in the House
of Representatives was hostile to him, and the
next election made this a majority. The first
indication of the shape which the opposition
was to take became visible in the vote in the
Senate upon confirming Mr. Clay as Secretary
of State. There were fourteen nays against
twenty-seven yeas, and an inspection of the
list showed that the South was beginning to
consolidate more closely than heretofore as a
sectional force in politics. The formation of
a Southern party distinctly organized in the
interests of slavery, already apparent in the
unanimity of the Southern Electoral Colleges
against Mr. Adams, thus received further illus-

tration; and the skilled eye of the President
noted "the rallying of the South and of Southern interests and prejudices to the men of the
South." It is possible now to see plainly that
Mr. Adams was really the first leader in the long
crusade against slavery; it was in opposition to
him that the South became a political unit; and
a true instinct taught him the trend of Southern
politics long before the Northern statesmen ap-
prehended it, perhaps before even any Southern
statesman had distinctly formulated it. This
new development in the politics of the country
soon received further illustration. The first
message which Mr. Adams had occasion to send
to Congress gave another opportunity to his ill-
wishers. Therein he stated that the invitation
which had been extended to the United States
to be represented at the Congress of Panama
had been accepted, and that he should commission ministers to attend the meeting. Neither
in matter nor in manner did this proposition
contain any just element of offence. It was
customary for the Executive to initiate new
missions simply by the nomination of envoys to
fill them; and in such case the Senate, if it did
not think the suggested mission desirable, could
simply decline to confirm the nomination upon
that ground. An example of this has been
already seen in the two nominations of Mr.

Adams himself to the Court of Russia in the Presidency of Mr. Madison. But now vehement assaults were made upon the President, alike in the Senate and in the House, on the utterly absurd ground that he had transcended his powers. Incredible, too, as it may seem at this day it was actually maintained that there was no occasion whatsoever for the United States to desire representation at such a gathering. Prolonged and bitter was the opposition which the Administration was compelled to encounter in a measure to which there so obviously ought to have been instant assent if considered solely upon its intrinsic merits, but upon which nevertheless the discussion actually overshadowed all other questions which arose during the session. The President had the good fortune to find the powerful aid of Mr. Webster enlisted in his behalf, and ultimately he prevailed; but it was of ill augury at this early date to see that personal hostility was so widespread and so rancorous that it could make such a prolonged and desperate resistance with only the faintest pretext of right as a basis for its action. Yet a great and fundamental cause of the feeling manifested lay hidden away beneath the surface in the instinctive antipathy of the slave-holders to Mr. Adams and all his thoughts, his ways, and his doings. For into this ques-

tion of countenancing the Panama Congress,
slavery and " the South " entered and imported
into a portion of the opposition a certain element of reasonableness and propriety in a political sense.   When we see the Southern statesmen banded against President Adams in these
debates, as we know the future which was hidden from them, it almost makes us believe that
their vindictiveness was justified by an instinctive forecasting of his character and his mission
in life, and that without knowing it they already felt the influence of the acts which he was
yet to do against them.   For the South, without present dread of an abolition movement, yet
hated this Panama Congress with a contemptuous loathing not alone because the South
American states had freed all slaves within
their limits, but because there was actually a
fair chance that Hayti would be admitted to
representation at the sessions as a sovereign
state.   That the President of the United States
should propose to send white citizens of that
country to sit cheek by jowl on terms of official equality with the revolted blacks of Hayti
fired the Southern heart with rage inexpres-
sible.   The proposition was a further infusion
of cement to aid in the Southern consolidation
so rapidly going forward, and was substantially
the beginning of the sense of personal aliena-

tion henceforth to grow steadily more bitter on
the part of the slaveholders towards Mr. Adams.
Without designing it he had struck the first
blow in a fight which was to absorb his energies
for the rest of his life.

Such evil forebodings as might too easily be
drawn from the course of this debate were soon
and amply fulfilled. The opposition increased
rapidly until when Congress came together in
December, 1827, it had attained overshadowing
proportions. Not only was a member of that
party elected Speaker of the House of Representatives, but a decided majority of both Houses
of Congress was arrayed against the Administration — " a state of things which had never
before occurred under the Government of the
United States." All the committees too were
composed of four opposition and only three
Administration members. With more exciting issues this relationship of the executive and
legislative departments might have resulted in
dangerous collisions ; but in this season of political quietude it only made the position of the
President extremely uncomfortable. Mr. Van
Buren soon became recognized as the formidable leader and organizer of the Jackson forces.
His capacity as a political strategist was so far
in advance of that of any other man of those
times that it might have secured success even

had he been encountered by tactics similar to
his own. But since on the contrary he had only
to meet straightforward simplicity, it was soon
apparent that he would have everything his
own way. It was disciplined troops against the
militia of honest merchants and farmers; and
the result was not to be doubted. Mr. Adams
and his friends were fond of comparing Van
Buren with Aaron Burr, though predicting that
he would be too shrewd to repeat Burr's blunders. From the beginning they declined to
meet with his own weapons a man whom they
so contemned. It was about this time that a
new nomenclature of parties was introduced into
our politics. The administrationists called themselves National Republicans, a name which in a
few years was changed for that of Whigs, while
the opposition or Jacksonians were known as
Democrats, a title which has been ever since
retained by the same party.

The story of Mr. Adams's Administration will
detain the historian, and even the biographer,
only a very short time. Not an event occurred
during those four years which appears of any
especial moment. Our foreign relations were
all pacific; and no grave crisis or great issue was
developed in domestic affairs. It was a period
of tranquillity, in which the nation advanced
rapidly in prosperity. For many years dulness

had reigned in business, but returning activity
was encouraged by the policy of the new Government, and upon all sides various industries
became active and thriving.   So far as the rule
of Mr. Adams was marked by any distinguish-
ing characteristic, it was by a care for the material welfare of the people.   More commercial
treaties were negotiated during his Administration than in the thirty-six years preceding his
inauguration.   He was a strenuous advocate of
internal improvements, and happily the condition of the national finances enabled the Government to embark in enterprises of this kind.
He suggested many more than were undertaken,
but not perhaps more than it would have been
quite possible to carry out.   He was always
chary of making a show of himself before the
people for the sake of gaining popularity.
When invited to attend the annual exhibition
of the Maryland Agricultural Society, shortly
after his inauguration, he declined, and wrote in
his Diary: " To gratify this wish I must give
four days of my time, no trifle of expense, and
set a precedent for being claimed as an article of
exhibition at all the cattle-shows throughout the
Union."   Other gatherings would prefer equally
reasonable demands, in responding to which
" some duty must be neglected."   But the opening of the Chesapeake and Ohio Canal was an

event sufficiently momentous and national in its character to justify the President's attendance. He was requested in the presence of a great concourse of people to dig the first shovelful of earth and to make a brief address. The speech-making was easy; but when the digging was to be done he encountered some unexpected obstacle and the soil did not yield to his repeated efforts. Not to be defeated, however, he stripped off his coat, went to work in earnest with the spade and raised the earth successfully. Naturally such readiness was hailed with loud applause and pleased the great crowd who saw it. But in Mr. Adams's career it was an exceptional occurrence that enabled him to conciliate a momentary popularity; it was seldom that he enjoyed or used an opportunity of gaining the cheap admiration or shallow friendship of the multitude.

At least one moral to be drawn from the story of Mr. Adams's Presidency perhaps deserves rather to be called an *immoral*, and certainly furnishes unwelcome support to those persons who believe that conscientiousness is out of place in politics. It has been said that no sooner was General Jackson fairly defeated than he was again before the people as a candidate for the next election. An opposition to the new Administration was in process of formation actually before there had been time for that Administra-

tion to declare, much less to carry out, any
policy or even any measure. The opposition
was therefore not one of principle; it was not
dislike of anything done or to be done; it did
not pretend to have a purpose of saving the
people from blunders or of offering them greater
advantages. It was simply an opposition, or
more properly an hostility, to the President and
his Cabinet, and was conducted by persons who
wished in as short a time as possible themselves
to control and fill those positions. The sole
ground upon which these opponents stood was,
that they would rather have General Jackson at
the head of affairs than Mr. Adams. The issue
was purely personal; it was so when the opposition first developed, and it remained so until
that opposition triumphed.

Under no circumstances can it be more excusable for an elective magistrate to seek personal good will towards himself than when his
rival seeks to supplant him simply on the basis
of enjoying a greater measure of such good will.
Had any important question of policy been dividing the people, it would have been easy for a
man of less moral courage and independence than
belonged to Mr. Adams to select the side which
he thought right, and to await the outcome at
least with constancy. But the only real question raised was this: will Mr. Adams or Gen-

eral Jackson — two individuals representing as
yet no antagonistic policies — be preferred by
the greater number of voters in 1829? If, however, there was no great apparent issue open between these two men, at least there was a very
wide difference between their characters, a point
of some consequence in a wholly personal com-
petition.   It is easy enough now to see how this
gaping difference displayed itself from the beginning, and how the advantage for winning
was throughout wholly on the side of Jackson.
The course to be pursued by Mr. Adams in order
to insure victory was obvious enough; being simply to secure the largest following and most
efficient support possible.   The arts by which
these objects were to be attained were not obscure nor beyond his power.   If he wished a
second term, as beyond question he did, two
methods were of certain utility.   He should
make the support of his Administration a source
of profit to the supporters; and he should conciliate good will by every means that offered.
To the former end what more efficient means
could be devised than a body of office-holders
owing their positions to his appointment and
likely to have the same term of office as himself?   His neglect to create such a corps of
stanch supporters cannot be explained on the
ground that so plain a scheme of perpetuating

power had not then been devised in the Republic. Mr. Jefferson had practised it, to an extent which now seems moderate, but which had been sufficiently extensive to deprive any successor of the honor of novelty in originating it. The times were ripe for it, and the nation would not have revolted at it, as was made apparent when General Jackson, succeeding Mr. Adams, at once carried out the system with a thoroughness that has never been surpassed, and with a success in achieving results so great that almost no politician has since failed to have recourse to the same practice. Suggestions and temptations, neither of which were wanting, were however alike thrown away upon Mr. Adams. Friendship or hostility to the President were the only two matters which were sure to have no effect whatsoever upon the fate of an incumbent or an aspirant. Scarcely any removals were made during his Administration, and every one of the few was based solely upon a proved unfitness of the official. As a consequence very few new appointments were made, and in every instance the appointee was, or was believed to be, the fittest man without regard to his political bias. This entire elimination of the question of party allegiance from every department of the public service was not a specious protestation, but an undeniable fact at which friends grum-

bled bitterly, and upon which foes counted often
with an ungenerous but always with an implicit
reliance. It was well known, for example, that
in the Customs Department there were many
more avowed opponents than supporters of the
Administration. What was to be thought, the
latter angrily asked, of a president who refused
to make any distinction between the sheep and
the goats? But while Mr. Adams, unmoved by
argument, anger, or entreaty, thus alienated
many and discouraged all, every one was made
acquainted with the antipodal principles of his
rival. The consequence was inevitable; many
abandoned Adams from sheer irritation; multi-
tudes became cool and indifferent concerning
him; the great number of those whose political
faith was so weak as to be at the ready command of their own interests, or the interests of
a friend or relative, yielded to a pressure against
which no counteracting force was employed. In
a word, no one who had not a strong and independent personal conviction in behalf of Mr.
Adams found the slightest inducement to belong
to his party. It did not require much political
sagacity to see that in quiet times, with no great
issue visibly at stake, a following thus composed
could not include a majority of the nation. It is
true that in fact there was opening an issue as
great as has ever been presented to the Ameri-

can people, — an issue between government conducted with a sole view to efficiency and honesty
and government conducted very largely, if not
exclusively, with a view to individual and party
ascendency.   The new system afterward inaugurated by General Jackson, directly opposite to
that of Mr. Adams and presenting a contrast to
it as wide as is to be found in history, makes
this fact glaringly plain to us.   But during the
years of Mr. Adams's Administration it was
dimly perceived only by a few.   Only one side
of the shield had then been shown.   The people
did not appreciate that Adams and Jackson
were representatives of two conflicting principles of administration which went to the very
basis of our system of government.   Had the
issue been as apparent and as well understood
then as it is now, in retrospect, the decision of
the nation might have been different.   But unfortunately the voters only beheld two individuals pitted against each other for the popular
suffrage, of whom one, a brilliant soldier, would
stand by and reward his friends, and the other,
an uninteresting civilian, ignored all distinction
between friend and foe.

It was not alone in the refusal to use patronage that Mr. Adams's rigid conscientiousness
showed itself.   He was equally obstinate in declining ever to stretch a point however slightly

in order to win the favor of any body of the
people whether large or small. He was warned
that his extensive schemes for internal improvement would alienate especially the important
State of Virginia. He could not of course be
expected to change his policy out of respect
to Virginian prejudices; but he was advised to
mitigate his expression of that policy, and to
some extent it was open to him to do so. But
he would not; his utterances went the full
length of his opinions, and he persistently urged
upon Congress many plans which he approved,
but which he could not have the faintest hopes
of seeing adopted. The consequence was that
he displeased Virginia. He notes the fact in
the Diary in the tone of one who endures persecution for righteousness' sake, and who means
to be very stubborn in his righteousness. Again
it was suggested to him to embody in one of his
messages " something soothing for South Carolina." But there stood upon the statute books
of South Carolina an unconstitutional law which
had greatly embarrassed the national government, and which that rebellious little State with
characteristic contumaciousness would not repeal. Under such circumstances, said Mr.
Adams, I have no " soothing " words for South
Carolina.

It was not alone by what he did and by what

he would not do that Mr. Adams toiled to insure the election of General Jackson far more
sedulously and efficiently than did the General
himself or any of his partisans. In most cases
it was probably the manner quite as much as
the act which made Mr. Adams unpopular. In
his anxiety to be upright he was undoubtedly
prone to be needlessly disagreeable. His uncompromising temper put on an ungracious aspect. His conscientiousness wore the appearance of offensiveness. The Puritanism in his
character was strongly tinged with that old New
England notion that whatever is disagreeable is
probably right, and that a painful refusal would
lose half its merit in being expressed courteously;
that a right action should never be done in a
pleasing way; not only that no pill should be
sugar-coated, but that the bitterest ingredient
should be placed on the outside. In repudiat-
ing attractive vices the Puritans had rejected
also those amenities which might have decently
concealed or even mildly decorated the forbidding angularities of a naked Virtue which certainly did not imitate the form of any goddess
who had ever before attracted followers. Mr.
Adams was a complete and thorough Puritan,
wonderfully little modified by times and circumstances. The ordinary arts of propitiation
would have appeared to him only a feeble and

diluted form of dishonesty; while suavity and graciousness of demeanor would have seemed as unbecoming to this rigid official as love-making or wine-bibbing seem to a strait-laced parson. It was inevitable, therefore, that he should never avert by his words any ill-will naturally caused by his acts; that he should never soothe disappointment, or attract calculating selfishness. He was an adept in alienation, a novice in conciliation. His magnetism was negative. He made few friends; and had no interested following whatsoever. No one was enthusiastic on his behalf; no band worked for him with the ardor of personal devotion. His party was composed of those who had sufficient intelligence to appreciate his integrity and sufficient honesty to admire it. These persons respected him, and when election day came they would vote for him; but they did not canvass zealously in his behalf, nor do such service for him as a very different kind of feeling induced the Jackson men to do for their candidate.[1] The fervid laborers in pol-

---

[1] Mr. Mills, in writing of Mr. Adams's inauguration, expressed well what many felt. "This same President of ours is a man that I can never court nor be on very familiar terms with. There is a cold, repulsive atmosphere about him that is too chilling for my respiration, and I shall certainly keep at a distance from its influence. I wish him God-speed in his Administration, and am heartily disposed to lend him my feeble aid whenever he may need it in a correct course; but he can-

itics left Mr. Adams alone in his chilling respectability, and went over to a camp where all scruples were consumed in the glowing heat of a campaign conducted upon the single and simple principle of securing victory.

Mr. Adams's relations with the members of his Cabinet were friendly throughout his term. Men of their character and ability, brought into daily contact with him, could not fail to appreciate and admire the purity of his motives and the patriotism of his conduct; nor was he wanting in a measure of consideration and deference towards them perhaps somewhat greater than might have been expected from him, sometimes even carried to the point of yielding his

not expect me to become his warm and devoted partisan." A like sentiment was expressed also much more vigorously by Ezekiel Webster to Daniel Webster, in a letter of February 15, 1829. The writer there attributes the defeat of Mr. Adams to personal dislike to him. People, he said, "always supported his cause from a cold sense of duty," and "we soon satisfy ourselves that we have discharged our duty to the cause of any man when we do not entertain for him one personal kind feeling, nor cannot unless we disembowel ourselves like a trussed turkey of all that is human nature within us." With a candidate "of popular character, like Mr. Clay," the result would have been different. "The measures of his [Adams's] Administration were just and wise and every honest man should have supported them, but many honest men did not for the reason I have mentioned." — *Webster's Private Correspondence*, vol. i. p. 469.

opinion in matters of consequence. It was his wish that the unity of the body should remain unbroken during his four years of office, and the wish was very nearly realized. Unfortunately, however, in his last year it became necessary for him to fill the mission to England, and Governor Barbour was extremely anxious for the place. It was already apparent that the coming election was likely to result in the succession of Jackson, and Mr. Adams notes that Barbour's extreme desire to receive the appointment was due to his wish to find a good harbor ere the approaching storm should burst. The remark was made without anger, in the tone of a man who had seen enough of the world not to expect too much from any of his fellow men; and the appointment was made, somewhat to the chagrin of Webster and Rush, either one of whom would have gladly accepted it. The vacancy thus caused, the only one which arose during his term, was filled by General Peter B. Porter, a gentleman whom Mr. Adams selected not as his own choice, but out of respect to the wishes of the Cabinet, and in order to "terminate the Administration in harmony with itself." The only seriously unpleasant occurrence was the treachery of Postmaster-General McLean, who saw fit to profess extreme devotion to Mr. Adams while secretly aiding General Jackson.

His perfidy was not undetected, and great pressure was brought to bear on the President to remove him. Mr. Adams, however, refused to do so, and McLean had the satisfaction of stepping from his post under Mr. Adams into a judgeship conferred by General Jackson, having shown his impartiality and judicial turn of mind, it is to be supposed, by declaring his warm allegiance to each master in turn.

The picture of President Adams's daily life is striking in its simplicity and its laboriousness. This chief magistrate of a great nation was wont to rise before daybreak, often at four or five o'clock even in winter, not unfrequently to build and light his own fire, and to work hard for hours when most persons in busy life were still comfortably slumbering. The forenoon and afternoon he devoted to public affairs, and often he complains that the unbroken stream of visitors gives him little opportunity for hard or continuous labor. Such work he was compelled to do chiefly in the evening; and he did not always make up for early hours of rising by a correspondingly early bedtime; though sometimes in the summer we find him going to bed between eight and nine o'clock, an hour which probably few Presidents have kept since then. He strove to care for his health by daily exercise. In the morning he swam in the Potomac,

often for a long time; and more than once he
encountered no small risk in this pastime. During the latter part of his Presidential term he
tried riding on horseback. At times when the
weather compelled him to walk, and business
was pressing, he used to get his daily modicum
of fresh air before the sun was up. A life of
this kind with more of hardship than of relaxation in it was ill fitted to sustain in robust
health a man sixty years of age, and it is not
surprising that Mr. Adams often complained of
feeling ill, dejected, and weary. Yet he never
spared himself, nor apparently thought his
habits too severe, and actually toward the close
of his term he spoke of his trying daily routine
as constituting a very agreeable life. He usually
began the day by reading " two or three chapters in the Bible with Scott's and Hewlett's
Commentaries," being always a profoundly reli-
gious man of the old-fashioned school then prevalent in New England.

It could hardly have added to the meagre
comforts of such a life to be threatened with
assassination. Yet this danger was thrust upon
Mr. Adams's attention upon one occasion at
least under circumstances which gave to it a
very serious aspect. The tranquillity with which
he went through the affair showed that his
physical courage was as imperturbable as his

moral. The risk was protracted throughout a considerable period, but he never let it disturb the even tenor of his daily behavior or warp his actions in the slightest degree, save only that when he was twice or thrice brought face to face with the intending assassin he treated the fellow with somewhat more curt brusqueness than was his wont. But when the danger was over he bore his would-be murderer no malice, and long afterward actually did him a kindly service.

Few men in public life have been subjected to trials of temper so severe as vexed Mr. Adams during his Presidential term. To play an intensely exciting game strictly in accordance with rigid moral rules of the player's own arbitrary enforcement, and which are utterly repudiated by a less scrupulous antagonist, can hardly tend to promote contentment and amiability. Neither are slanders and falsehoods mollifying applications to a statesman inspired with an upright and noble ambition. Mr. Adams bore such assaults, ranging from the charge of having corruptly bought the Presidency down to that of being a Freemason with such grim stoicism as he could command. The disappearance and probable assassination of Morgan at this time led to a strong feeling throughout the country

against Freemasonry, and the Jackson men at
once proclaimed abroad that Adams was one of
the brotherhood, and offered, if he should deny
it, to produce the records of the lodge to which
he belonged. The allegation was false ; he was
not a Mason, and his friends urged him to say
so publicly ; but he replied bitterly that his
denial would probably at once be met by a complete set of forged records of a fictitious lodge,
and the people would not know whom to believe. Next he was said to have bargained for
the support of Daniel Webster, by promising
to distribute offices to Federalists. This accusation was a cruel perversion of his very virtues ;
for its only foundation lay in the fact that in
the venturesome but honorable attempt to be
President of a nation rather than of a party,
he had in some instances given offices to old
Federalists, certainly with no hope or possibility of reconciling to himself the almost useless
wreck of that now powerless and shrunken
party, one of whose liveliest traditions was
hatred of him. Stories were even set afloat
that some of his accounts, since he had been
in the public service, were incorrect. But the
most extraordinary and ridiculous tale of all
was that during his residence in Russia he had
prostituted a beautiful American girl, whom he
then had in his service, in order " to seduce the

passions of the Emperor Alexander and sway
him to political purposes."

These and other like provocations were not
only discouraging but very irritating, and Mr.
Adams was not of that careless disposition
which is little affected by unjust accusation.
On the contrary he was greatly incensed by
such treatment, and though he made the most
stern and persistent effort to endure an inevitable trial with a patience born of philosophy,
since indifference was not at his command, yet
he could not refrain from the expression of his
sentiments in his secret communings.   Occasionally he allowed his wrath to explode with
harmless violence between the covers of the
Diary, and doubtless he found relief while he
discharged his fierce diatribes on these private
sheets.   His vituperative power was great, and
some specimens of it may not come amiss in a
sketch of the man.   The senators who did not
call upon him he regarded as of "rancorous
spirit."   He spoke of the falsehoods and misre-
presentations which "the skunks of party slander
. . . have been . . . squirting round the House
of Representatives, thence to issue and perfume
the atmosphere of the Union."   His most intense hatred and vehement denunciation were
reserved for John Randolph, whom he thought
an abomination too odious and despicable to be

described in words, "the image and superscription of a great man stamped upon base metal." "The besotted violence" of Randolph, he said, has deprived him of "all right to personal civility from me;" and certainly this excommunication from courtesy was made complete and effective. He speaks again of the same victim as a "frequenter of gin lane and beer alley." He indignantly charges that Calhoun, as Speaker, permitted Randolph "in speeches of ten hours long to drink himself drunk with bottled porter, and in raving balderdash of the meridian of Wapping to revile the absent and the present, the living and the dead." This, he says, was "tolerated by Calhoun, because Randolph's ribaldry was all pointed against the Administration, especially against Mr. Clay and me." Again he writes of Randolph: "The rancor of this man's soul against me is that which sustains his life: the agony of [his] envy and hatred of me, and the hope of effecting my downfall, are [his] chief remaining sources of vitality. The issue of the Presidential election will kill [him] by the gratification of [his] revenge." So it was also with W. B. Giles, of Virginia. But Giles's abuse was easier to bear since it had been poured in torrents upon every reputable man, from Washington downwards, who had been prominent in public affairs since the adoption of the Constitution, so that Giles's memory is now preserved from oblivion solely by the connection which he established with the great and honorable statesmen of the Republic by a course of ceaseless attacks upon them. Some of the foregoing expressions of Mr. Adams may be open to objection on the score of good taste; but the provocation was extreme; public retaliation he would not practise, and wrath must sometimes burst forth in language which was not so unusual in that day as it is at present. It is an unquestionable fact, of which the credit to Mr. Adams can hardly be exaggerated, that he never in any single instance found an excuse for an unworthy act on his own part in the fact that competitors or adversaries were resorting to such expedients.

The election of 1828 gave 178 votes for Jackson and only 83 for Adams. Calhoun was continued as Vice-President by 171 votes, showing plainly enough that even yet there were not two political parties, in any customary or proper sense of the phrase. The victory of Jackson had been foreseen by every one. What had been so generally anticipated could not take Mr. Adams by surprise; yet it was idle for him to seek to conceal his disappointment that an Administration which he had conducted with his best ability and with thorough conscientiousness should not have seemed to the people worthy of continuance for another term. Little suspecting what the future had in store for him, he felt that his public career had culminated and probably had closed forever, and that if it had not closed exactly in disgrace, yet at least it could not be regarded as ending gloriously or even satisfactorily. But he summoned all his philosophy and fortitude to his aid; he fell back upon his clear conscience and comported himself with dignity, showing all reasonable courtesy to his successor and only perhaps seeming a little deficient in filial piety in presenting so striking a contrast to the shameful conduct of his father in a like crucial hour. His retirement brought to a close a list of Presidents who deserved to be called statesmen in the highest sense of that term, honorable men, pure patriots, and, with perhaps one exception, all of the first order of ability in public affairs. It is necessary to come far down towards this day before a worthy successor of those great men is met with in the list. Dr. Von Holst, by far the ablest writer who has yet dealt with American history, says: " In the person of Adams the last statesman who was to occupy it for a long time left the White House." General Jackson, the candidate of the populace and the representative hero of the ignorant masses, instituted a new system of administering the Government in which personal interests became the most important element, and that organization and strategy were developed which have since become known and infamous under the name of the "political machine."

While Mr. Adams bore his defeat like a philosopher, he felt secretly very depressed and unhappy by reason of it. He speaks of it as leaving his "character and reputation a wreck," and says that the "sun of his political life sets in the deepest gloom." On January 1, 1829, he writes: "The year begins in gloom. My wife had a sleepless and painful night. The dawn was overcast, and as I began to write my shaded lamp went out, self-extinguished. It was only for lack of oil, and the notice of so trivial an incident may serve but to mark the present temper of my mind." It is painful to behold a man of his vigor, activity, and courage thus prostrated. Again he writes : —

"Three days more and I shall be restored to private life, and left to an old age of retirement though certainly not of repose. I go into it with a combination of parties and public men against my character and reputation, such as I believe never before was exhibited against any man since this Union existed. Posterity will scarcely believe it, but so it is, that this

combination against me has been formed and is now
exulting in triumph over me, for the devotion of my
life and of all the faculties of my soul to the Union,
and to the improvement, physical, moral, and intellectual of my country."

Melancholy words these to be written by an
old man who had worked so hard and been so
honest, and whose ambition had been of the
kind that ennobles him who feels it! Could the
curtain of the future have been lifted but for
a moment what relief would the glimpse have
brought to his crushed and wearied spirit. But
though coming events may cast shadows before
them, they far less often send bright rays in advance. So he now resolved "to go into the
deepest retirement and withdraw from all connection with public affairs." Yet it was with
regret that he foretold this fate, and he looked
forward with solicitude to the effect which such
a mode of life, newly entered upon at his age,
would have upon his mind and character. He
hopes rather than dares to predict that he will
be provided "with useful and profitable occupation, engaging so much of his thoughts and feelings that his mind may not be left to corrode
itself."

His return to Quincy held out the less promise of comfort, because the old chasm between
him and the Federalist gentlemen of Boston had

been lately reopened.   Certain malicious newspaper paragraphs, born of the mischievous spirit
of the wretched Giles, had recently set afloat
some stories designed seriously to injure Mr. Adams.   These were, substantially, that in 1808–9
he had been convinced that some among the
leaders of the Federalist party in New England were entertaining a project for separation
from the Union, that he had feared that this
event would be promoted by the embargo, that
he foresaw that the seceding portion would inevitably be compelled into some sort of alliance
with Great Britain, that he suspected negotiations to this end to have been already set on
foot, that he thereupon gave privately some
more or less distinct intimations of these notions of his to sundry prominent Republicans,
and even to President Jefferson.   These tales,
much distorted from the truth and exaggerated
as usual, led to the publication of an open letter,
in November, 1828, addressed by thirteen Federalists of note in Massachusetts to John Quincy
Adams, demanding names and specifications and
the production of evidence.   Mr. Adams replied
briefly, with dignity, and, considering the circumstances, with good temper, stating fairly the
substantial import of what he had really said,
declaring that he had never mentioned names,
and refusing, for good reasons given, either to

do so now or to publish the grounds of such
opinions as he had entertained. It was sufficiently clear that he had said nothing secretly
which he had reason to regret; and that if he
sought to shun the discussion opened by his adversaries, he was influenced by wise forbearance,
and not at all by any fear of the consequences
to himself. A dispassionate observer could
have seen that behind this moderate, rather de-
precatory letter there was an abundant reserve
of controversial material held for the moment
in check. But his adversaries were not dispassionate; on the contrary they were greatly excited and were honestly convinced of the perfect
goodness of their cause. They were men of
the highest character in public and private life,
deservedly of the best repute in the community,
of unimpeachable integrity in motives and dealings, influential and respected, men whom it was
impossible in New England to treat with neglect or indifference. For this reason it was only
the harder to remain silent beneath their published reproach when a refutation was possible.
Hating Mr. Adams with an animosity not diminished by the lapse of years since his defection
from their party, strong in a consciousness of
their own standing before their fellow citizens,
the thirteen notables responded with much ac-
rimony to Mr. Adams's unsatisfactory letter.

Thus persistently challenged and assailed, at a
time when his recent crushing political defeat
made an attack upon him seem a little ungenerous, Mr. Adams at last went into the fight
in earnest. He had the good fortune to be
thoroughly right, and also to have sufficient
evidence to prove and justify at least as much
as he had ever said. All this evidence he
brought together in a vindicatory pamphlet,
which, however, by the time he had completed
it he decided not to publish. But fortunately
he did not destroy it, and his grandson, in the
exercise of a wise discretion, has lately given it
to the world. His foes never knew how deeply
they were indebted to the self-restraint which
induced him to keep this formidable missive
harmless in his desk. Full of deep feeling, yet
free from ebullitions of temper, clear in statement, concise in style, conclusive in facts, un-
answerable in argument, unrelentingly severe
in dealing with opponents, it is as fine a specimen of political controversy as exists in the
language. Its historical value cannot be exaggerated, but apart from this as a mere literary production it is admirable. Happy were
the thirteen that they one and all went down to
their graves complaisantly thinking that they
had had the last word in the quarrel, little suspecting how great was their obligation to Mr.

Adams for having granted them that privilege. One would think that they might have writhed beneath their moss-grown headstones on the day when his last word at length found public utterance, albeit that the controversy had then become one of the dusty tales of history.[1]

But this task of writing a demolishing pamphlet against the prominent gentlemen of the neighborhood to which he was about to return for his declining years could hardly have been a grateful task. The passage from political disaster to social enmities could not but be painful; and Mr. Adams was probably never more unhappy than at this period of his life. The reward which virtue was tendering to him seemed unmixed bitterness.

Thus at the age of sixty-two years, Mr. Adams found himself that melancholy product of the American governmental system — an ex-

[1] It is with great reluctance that these comments are made, since some persons may think that they come with ill grace from one whose grandfather was one of the thirteen and was supposed to have drafted one or both of their letters. But in spite of the prejudice naturally growing out of this fact, a thorough study of the whole subject has convinced me that Mr. Adams was unquestionably and completely right, and I have no escape from saying so. His adversaries had the excuse of honesty in political error — an excuse which the greatest and wisest men must often fall back upon in times of hot party warfare.

President. At this stage it would seem that the
fruit ought to drop from the bough, no further
process of development being reasonably probable for it.   Yet Mr. Adams had by no means
reached this measure of ripeness; he still enjoyed abundant vigor of mind and body, and to
lapse into dignified decrepitude was not agreeable, indeed was hardly possible for him.   The
prospect gave him profound anxiety; he dreaded
idleness, apathy, and decay with a keen terror
which perhaps constituted a sufficient guaranty
against them.   Yet what could he do?   It would
be absurd for him now to furbish up the rusty
weapons of the law and enter again upon the
tedious labor of collecting a clientage.   His
property was barely sufficient to enable him to
live respectably, even according to the simple
standard of the time, and could open to him no
occupation in the way of gratifying unremuner-
ative tastes.   In March, 1828, he had been advised to use five thousand dollars in a way to
promote his reëlection.   He refused at once,
upon principle; but further set forth " candidly,
the state of his affairs : " —

" All my real estate in Quincy and Boston is mort-
gaged for the payment of my debts ; the income of
my whole private estate is less than $6,000 a year,
and I am paying at least two thousand of that for interest on my debt.   Finally, upon going out of office

in one year from this time, destitute of all means of acquiring property, it will only be by the sacrifice of that which I now possess that I shall be able to support my family."

At first he plunged desperately into the Latin classics. He had a strong taste for such reading, and he made a firm resolve to compel this taste now to stand him in good stead in his hour of need. He courageously demanded solace from a pursuit which had yielded him pleasure enough in hours of relaxation, but which was altogether inadequate to fill the huge vacuum now suddenly created in his time and thoughts. There is much pathos in this spectacle of the old man setting himself with ever so feeble a weapon, yet with stern determination, to conquer the cruelty of circumstances. But he knew, of course, that the Roman authors could only help him for a time, by way of distraction, in carrying him through a transition period. He soon set more cheerfully at work upon a memoir of his father, and had also plans for writing a history of the United States. Literature had always possessed strong charms for him, and he had cultivated it after his usual studious and conscientious fashion. But his style was too often prolix, sententious, and turgid — faults which marked nearly all the writing done in this country in those days. The

world has probably not lost much by reason of
the non-completion of the contemplated volumes.
He could have made no other contribution to
the history of the country at all approaching
in value or interest to the Diary, of which a
most important part was still to be written.
For a brief time just now this loses its historic
character, but makes up for the loss by depicting
admirably some traits in the mental constitution of the diarist. Tales of enchantment, he
says, pleased his boyhood, but " the humors of
Falstaff hardly affected me at all. Bardolph
and Pistol and Nym were personages quite un-
intelligible to me ; and the lesson of Sir Hugh
Evans to the boy Williams was quite too serious
an affair." In truth, no man can ever have
been more utterly void of a sense of humor or
an appreciation of wit than was Mr. Adams.
Not a single instance of an approach to either is
to be found throughout the twelve volumes of
his Diary. Not even in the simple form of the
" good story" could he find pleasure, and subtler
delicacies were wasted on his well-regulated
mind as dainty French dishes would be on the
wholesome palate of a day-laborer. The books
which bore the stamp of well-established approval, the acknowledged classics of the English, Latin, and French languages he read with
a mingled sense of duty and of pleasure, and

evidently with cultivated appreciation, though whether he would have made an original discovery of their merits may be doubted. Occasionally he failed to admire even those volumes which deserved admiration, and then with characteristic honesty he admitted the fact. He tried Paradise Lost ten times before he could get through with it, and was nearly thirty years old when he first succeeded in reading it to the end. Thereafter he became very fond of it, but plainly by an acquired taste. He tried smoking and Milton, he says, at the same time, in the hope of discovering the " recondite charm " in them which so pleased his father. He was more easily successful with the tobacco than with the poetry. Many another has had the like experience, but the confession is not always so frankly forthcoming.

Fate, however, had in store for Mr. Adams labors to which he was better suited than those of literature, and tasks to be performed which the nation could ill afford to exchange for an apotheosis of our second President, or even for a respectable but probably not very readable history. The most brilliant and glorious years of his career were yet to be lived. He was to earn in his old age a noble fame and distinction far transcending any achievement of his youth and middle age, and was to attain the highest pinnacle of his fame after he had left the greatest office of the Government, and during a period for which presumably nothing better had been allotted than that he should tranquilly await the summons of death.   It is a striking circumstance that the fullness of greatness for one who had been Senator, Minister to England, Secretary of State, and President, remained to be won in the comparatively humble position of a Representative in Congress.

CHAPTER III

IN September, 1830, Mr. Adams notes in his Diary a suggestion made to him that he might if he wished be elected to the national House of Representatives from the Plymouth district. The gentleman who threw out this tentative proposition remarked that in his opinion the acceptance of this position by an ex-President "instead of degrading the individual would elevate the representative character." Mr. Adams replied, that he "had in that respect no scruple whatever. No person could be degraded by serving the people as a Representative in Congress. Nor in my opinion would an ex-President of the United States be degraded by serving as a selectman of his town, if elected thereto by the people." A few weeks later his election was accomplished by a flattering vote, the poll showing for him 1817 votes out of 2565, with only 373 for the next candidate. He continued thenceforth to represent this district until his death, a period of about sixteen years. During this time he was occasionally suggested as a candidate for the governorship of the State, but was always reluctant to stand. The feeling between the Freemasons and the anti-Masons ran very high for several years, and once he was prevailed upon to allow his name to be used by the latter party. The result was that there was no election by the people; and as he had been very loath to enter the contest in the beginning, he insisted upon withdrawing from before the legislature. We have now therefore only to pursue his career in the lower house of Congress.

Unfortunately, but of obvious necessity, it is possible to touch only upon the more salient points of this which was really by far the most striking and distinguished portion of his life. To do more than this would involve an explanation of the politics of the country and the measures before Congress much more elaborate than would be possible in this volume. It will be necessary, therefore, to confine ourselves to drawing a picture of him in his character as the great combatant of Southern slavery. In the waging of this mighty conflict we shall see both his mind and his character developing in strength even in these years of his old age, and his traits standing forth in bolder relief than ever before. In his place on the floor of the House of Representatives he was destined to appear a more impressive figure than in any

of the higher positions which he had previously
filled.   There he was to do his greatest work
and to win a peculiar and distinctive glory
which takes him out of the general throng even
of famous statesmen, and entitles his name to be
remembered with an especial reverence.   Ade-
quately to sketch his achievements, and so to
do his memory the honor which it deserves,
would require a pen as eloquent as has been
wielded by any writer of our language.   I can
only attempt a brief and insufficient narrative.

In his conscientious way he was faithful and
industrious to a rare degree.   He was never absent and seldom late ; he bore unflinchingly the
burden of severe committee work, and shirked
no toil on the plea of age or infirmity.   He attended closely to all the business of the House ;
carefully formed his opinions on every question ;
never failed to vote except for cause ; and always
had a sufficient reason independent of party allegiance to sustain his vote.   Living in the age
of oratory, he earned the name of " the old man
eloquent."   Yet he was not an orator in the
sense in which Webster, Clay, and Calhoun
were orators.   He was not a rhetorician ; he had
neither grace of manner nor a fine presence,
neither an imposing delivery, nor even pleasing
tones.   On the contrary, he was exceptionally

lacking in all these qualities. He was short, rotund, and bald; about the time when he entered Congress, complaints become frequent in his Diary of weak and inflamed eyes, and soon these organs became so rheumy that the water would trickle down his cheeks; a shaking of the hand grew upon him to such an extent that in time he had to use artificial assistance to steady it for writing; his voice was high, shrill, liable to break, piercing enough to make itself heard, but not agreeable. This hardly seems the picture of an orator; nor was it to any charm of elocution that he owed his influence, but rather to the fact that men soon learned that what he said was always well worth hearing. When he entered Congress he had been for much more than a third of a century zealously gathering knowledge in public affairs, and during his career in that body every year swelled the already vast accumulation. Moreover, listeners were always sure to get a bold and an honest utterance and often pretty keen words from him, and he never spoke to an inattentive audience or to a thin house. Whether pleased or incensed by what he said, the Representatives at least always listened to it. He was by nature a hard fighter, and by the circumstances of his course in Congress this quality was stimulated to such a degree that parliamentary history does not show

his equal as a gladiator. His power of invective was extraordinary, and he was untiring and
merciless in his use of it. Theoretically he
disapproved of sarcasm, but practically he could
not refrain from it. Men winced and cowered
before his milder attacks, became sometimes
dumb, sometimes furious with mad rage before
his fiercer assaults. Such struggles evidently
gave him pleasure, and there was scarce a back
in Congress that did not at one time or another
feel the score of his cutting lash; though it was
the Southerners and the Northern allies of
Southerners whom chiefly he singled out for
torture. He was irritable and quick to wrath;
he himself constantly speaks of the infirmity of
his temper, and in his many conflicts his principal concern was to keep it in control. His
enemies often referred to it and twitted him
with it. Of alliances he was careless, and friendships he had almost none. But in the creation
of enmities he was terribly successful. Not so
much at first, but increasingly as years went on,
a state of ceaseless, vigilant hostility became his
normal condition. From the time when he fairly
entered upon the long struggle against slavery,
he enjoyed few peaceful days in the House.
But he seemed to thrive upon the warfare, and
to be never so well pleased as when he was
bandying hot words with slave-holders and the

Northern supporters of slave - holders. When
the air of the House was thick with crimination
and abuse he seemed to suck in fresh vigor and
spirit from the hate-laden atmosphere. When
invective fell around him in showers, he screamed
back his retaliation with untiring rapidity and
marvellous dexterity of aim. No odds could
appall him. With his back set firm against a
solid moral principle, it was his joy to strike
out at a multitude of foes. They lost their
heads as well as their tempers, but in the ex-
tremest moments of excitement and anger Mr.
Adams's brain seemed to work with machine-
like coolness and accuracy. With flushed face,
streaming eyes, animated gesticulation, and
cracking voice, he always retained perfect mas-
tery of all his intellectual faculties. He thus
became a terrible antagonist, whom all feared,
yet fearing could not refrain from attacking, so
bitterly and incessantly did he choose to exert
his wonderful power of exasperation. Few men
could throw an opponent into wild blind fury
with such speed and certainty as he could ; and
he does not conceal the malicious gratification
which such feats brought to him. A leader of
such fighting capacity, so courageous, with such
a magazine of experience and information, and
with a character so irreproachable, could have
won brilliant victories in public life at the head

of even a small band of devoted followers. But
Mr. Adams never had and apparently never
wanted followers. Other prominent public men
were brought not only into collision but into
comparison with their contemporaries. But Mr.
Adams's individuality was so strong that he can
be compared with no one. It was not an individuality of genius nor to any remarkable extent
of mental qualities ; but rather an individuality
of character. To this fact is probably to be
attributed his peculiar solitariness. Men touch
each other for purposes of attachment through
their characters much more than through their
minds. But few men, even in agreeing with Mr.
Adams, felt themselves in sympathy with him.
Occasionally conscience, or invincible logic, or
even policy and self-interest, might compel one
or another politician to stand beside him in
debate or in voting; but no current of fellow
feeling ever passed between such temporary
comrades and him. It was the cold connection
of duty or of business. The first instinct of
nearly every one was opposition towards him :
coalition might be forced by circumstances but
never came by volition. For the purpose of
winning immediate successes this was of course
a most unfortunate condition of relationships.
Yet it had some compensations : it left such
influence as Mr. Adams could exert by stead-

fastness and argument entirely unweakened by
suspicion of hidden motives or personal ends.
He had the weight and enjoyed the respect
which a sincerity beyond distrust must always
command in the long run.   Of this we shall see
some striking instances.

One important limitation, however, belongs to
this statement of solitariness.   It was confined
to his position in Congress.   Outside of the city
of Washington great numbers of the people,
especially in New England, lent him a hearty
support and regarded him with friendship and
admiration.   These men had strong convictions
and deep feelings, and their adherence counted
for much.   Moreover, their numbers steadily
increased, and Mr. Adams saw that he was the
leader in a cause which engaged the sound sense
and the best feeling of the intelligent people of
the country, and which was steadily gaining
ground.   Without such encouragement it is
doubtful whether even his persistence would
have held out through so long and extreme a
trial.   The sense of human fellowship was need-
ful to him ; he could go without it in Congress,
but he could not have gone without it altogether.

Mr. Adams took his seat in the House as a
member of the twenty-second Congress in December, 1831.   He had been elected by the National Republican, afterward better known as

the Whig party, but one of his first acts was to declare that he would be bound by no partisan connection, but would in every matter act independently. This course he regarded as a "duty imposed upon him by his peculiar position," in that he "had spent the greatest portion of his life in the service of the whole nation and had been honored with their highest trust." Many persons had predicted that he would find himself subjected to embarrassments and perhaps to humiliations by reason of his apparent descent in the scale of political dignities. He notes, however, that he encountered no annoyance on this score, but on the contrary he was rather treated with an especial respect. He was made chairman of the Committee on Manufactures, a laborious as well as an important and honorable position at all times, and especially so at this juncture when the rebellious mutterings of South Carolina against the protective tariff were already to be heard rolling and swelling like portentous thunder from the fiery Southern regions. He would have preferred to exchange this post for a place upon the Committee on Foreign Affairs, for whose business he felt more fitted. But he was told that in the impending crisis his ability, authority, and prestige were all likely to be needed in the place allotted to him to aid in the salvation of the country.

The nullification chapter of our history cannot here be entered upon at length, and Mr. Adams's connection with it must be very shortly stated. At the first meeting of his committee he remarks : " A reduction of the duties upon many of the articles in the tariff was understood by all to be the object to be effected ; " and a little later he said that he should be disposed to give such aid as he could to any plan for this reduction which the Treasury Department should devise. " He should certainly not consent to sacrifice the manufacturing interest," he said, " but something of concession would be due from that interest to appease the discontents of the South." He was in a reasonable frame of mind ; but unfortunately other people were rapidly ceasing to be reasonable. When Jackson's message of December 4, 1832, was promulgated, showing a disposition to do for South Carolina pretty much all that she demanded, Mr. Adams was bitterly indignant. The message, he said, " recommends a total change in the policy of the Union with reference to the Bank, manufactures, internal improvement, and the public lands. It goes to dissolve the Union into its original elements, and is in substance a complete surrender to the nullifiers of South Carolina." When, somewhat later on, the President lost his temper and flamed out in his famous proclamation to meet the nullification ordinance, he spoke in tones more pleasing to Mr. Adams. But the ultimate compromise which disposed of the temporary dissension without permanently settling the fundamental question of the constitutional right of nullification was extremely distasteful to him. He was utterly opposed to the concessions which were made while South Carolina still remained contumacious. He was for compelling her to retire altogether from her rebellious position and to repeal her unconstitutional enactments wholly and unconditionally, before one jot should be abated from the obnoxious duties. When the bill for the modification of the tariff was under debate, he moved to strike out all but the enacting clause, and supported his motion in a long speech, insisting that no tariff ought to pass until it was known "whether there was any measure by which a State could defeat the laws of the Union." In a minority report from his own committee he strongly censured the policy of the Administration. He was for meeting, fighting out, and determining at this crisis the whole doctrine of state rights and secession. "One particle of compromise," he said, with what truth events have since shown clearly enough, would "directly lead to the final and irretrievable dissolution of the Union."

In his usual strong and thorough-going fashion he was for persisting in the vigorous and spirited measures, the mere brief declaration of which, though so quickly receded from, won for Jackson a measure of credit greater than he deserved. Jackson was thrown into a great rage by the threats of South Carolina, and replied to them with the same prompt wrath with which he had sometimes resented insults from individuals. But in his cool inner mind he was in sympathy with the demands which that State preferred, and though undoubtedly he would have fought her, had the dispute been forced to that pass, yet he was quite willing to make concessions, which were in fact in consonance with his own views as well as with hers, in order to avoid that sad conclusion. He was satisfied to have the instant emergency pass over in a manner rendered superficially creditable to himself by his outburst of temper, under cover of which he sacrificed the substantial matter of principle without a qualm. He shook his fist and shouted defiance in the face of the nullifiers, while Mr. Clay smuggled a comfortable concession into their pockets. Jackson, notwithstanding his belligerent attitude, did all he could to help Clay and was well pleased with the result. Mr. Adams was not. He watched the disingenuous game with disgust. It is certain that if he had

still been in the White House, the matter would
have had a very different ending, bloodier, it
may be, and more painful, but much more conclusive.

For the most part Mr. Adams found himself
in opposition to President Jackson's Administration. This was not attributable to any sense
of personal hostility towards a successful rival,
but to an inevitable antipathy towards the
measures, methods, and ways adopted by the
General so unfortunately transferred to civil
life. Few intelligent persons, and none having
the statesman habit of mind, befriended the reckless, violent, eminently unstatesmanlike President. His ultimate weakness in the nullification
matter, his opposition to internal improvements,
his policy of sacrificing the public lands to individual speculators, his warfare against the Bank
of the United States conducted by methods the
most unjustifiable, the transaction of the removal
of the deposits so disreputable and injurious in
all its details, the importation of Mrs. Eaton's
visiting-list into the politics and government of
the country, the dismissal of the oldest and best
public servants as a part of the nefarious system of using public offices as rewards for political aid and personal adherence, the formation
from base ingredients of the ignoble " Kitchen
Cabinet," — all these doings, together with much

more of the like sort, constituted a career which
could only seem blundering, undignified, and dis-
honorable in the eyes of a man like Mr. Adams,
who regarded statesmanship with the reverence
due to the noblest of human callings.

Right as Mr. Adams was generally in his opposition to Jackson, yet once he deserves credit
for the contrary course. This was in the matter
of our relations with France. The treaty of
1831 secured to this country an indemnity of
$5,000,000, which, however, it had never been
possible to collect. This procrastination raised
Jackson's ever ready ire, and casting to the
winds any further dunning, he resolved either
to have the money or to fight for it. He sent
a message to Congress, recommending that if
France should not promptly settle the account,
letters of marque and reprisal against her commerce should be issued. He ordered Edward
Livingston, minister at Paris, to demand his
passports and cross over to London. These
eminently proper and ultimately effectual measures alarmed the large party of the timid; and
the General found himself in danger of extensive desertions even on the part of his usual
supporters. But as once before in a season of
his dire extremity his courage and vigor had
brought the potent aid of Mr. Adams to his
side, so now again he came under a heavy debt

of gratitude to the same champion.   Mr. Adams
stood by him with generous gallantry, and by a
telling speech in the House probably saved him
from serious humiliation and even disaster.   The
President's style of dealing had roused Mr.
Adams's spirit, and he spoke with a fire and
vehemence which accomplished the unusual feat
of changing the predisposed minds of men too
familiar with speech-making to be often much
influenced by it in the practical matter of voting.   He thought at the time that the success of
this speech, brilliant as it appeared, was not un-
likely to result in his political ruin.   Jackson
would befriend and reward his thorough-going
partisans at any cost to his own conscience or
the public welfare ; but the exceptional aid, tendered not from a sense of personal fealty to himself, but simply from the motive of aiding the
right cause happening in the especial instance
to have been espoused by him, never won from
him any token of regard.   In November, 1837,
Mr. Adams, speaking of his personal relations
with the President, said : —

"Though I had served him more than any other
living man ever did, and though I supported his Administration at the hazard of my own political destruction, and effected for him at a moment when his
own friends were deserting him what no other member of Congress ever accomplished for him — an

unanimous vote of the House of Representatives to
support him in his quarrel with France; though I
supported him in other very critical periods of his
Administration, my return from him was insult, indignity, and slander."

Antipathy had at last become the definitive
condition of these two men — antipathy both
political and personal. At one time a singular
effort to reconcile them — probably though not
certainly undertaken with the knowledge of
Jackson — was made by Richard M. Johnson.
This occurred shortly before the inauguration
of the war conducted by the President against
the Bank of the United States; and judging by
the rest of Jackson's behavior at this period,
there was probably at least as much of calcula-
tion in his motives, if in fact he was cognizant
of Johnson's approaches, as there was of any
real desire to reëstablish the bygone relation of
honorable friendship. To the advances thus
made Mr. Adams replied a little coldly, not
quite repellently, that Jackson, having been responsible for the suspension of personal intercourse, must now be undisguisedly the active
party in renewing it. At the same time he pro-
fessed himself "willing to receive in a spirit of
conciliation any advance which in that spirit
General Jackson might make." But nothing
came of this intrinsically hopeless attempt. On

the contrary the two drew rapidly and more widely apart, and entertained concerning each other opinions which grew steadily more unfavorable, and upon Adams's part more contemptuous, as time went on.

Fifteen months later General Jackson made his visit to Boston, and it was proposed that Harvard College should confer upon him the degree of Doctor of Laws. The absurdity of the act, considered simply in itself, was admitted by all. But the argument in its favor was based upon the established usage of the College as towards all other Presidents, so that its omission in this case might seem a personal slight. Mr. Adams, being at the time a member of the Board of Overseers, strongly opposed the proposition, but of course in vain. All that he could do was, for his own individual part, to refuse to be present at the conferring of the degree, giving as the minor reason for his absence, that he could hold no friendly intercourse with the President, but for the major reason that " independent of that, as myself an affectionate child of our Alma Mater, I would not be present to witness her disgrace in conferring her highest literary honors upon a barbarian who could not write a sentence of grammar and hardly could spell his own name." " A Doctorate of Laws," he said, " for which an apology was necessary,

was a cheap honor and . . . a sycophantic compliment." After the deed was done, he used to
amuse himself by speaking of " Doctor Andrew
Jackson." This same eastern tour of Jackson's
called forth many other expressions of bitter
sarcasm from Adams. The President was ill
and unable to carry out the programme of en-
tertainment and exhibition prepared for him:
whereupon Mr. Adams remarks : —

"I believe much of his debility is politic. . . . He
is one of our tribe of great men who turn disease to
commodity, like John Randolph, who for forty years
was always dying. Jackson, ever since he became a
mark of public attention, has been doing the same
thing. . . . He is now alternately giving out his
chronic diarrhœa and making Warren bleed him for a
pleurisy, and posting to Cambridge for a doctorate of
laws ; mounting the monument of Bunker's Hill to
hear a fulsome address and receive two cannon balls
from Edward Everett," etc. " Four fifths of his sick-
ness is trickery, and the other fifth mere fatigue."

This sounds, it must be confessed, a trifle
rancorous ; but Adams had great excuse for
nourishing rancor towards Jackson.

It is time, however, to return to the House
of Representatives. It was not by bearing his
share in the ordinary work of that body, important or exciting as that might at one time or
another happen to be, that Mr. Adams was to

win in Congress that reputation which has been
already described as far overshadowing all his
previous career. A special task and a peculiar
mission were before him. It was a part of his
destiny to become the champion of the anti-
slavery cause in the national legislature. Almost the first thing which he did after he had
taken his seat in Congress was to present "fifteen petitions signed numerously by citizens
of Pennsylvania, praying for the abolition of
slavery and the slave-trade in the District of
Columbia." He simply moved their reference
to the Committee on the District of Columbia,
declaring that he should not support that part
of the petition which prayed for abolition in
the District. The time had not yet come when
the South felt much anxiety at such manifestations, and these first stones were dropped into
the pool without stirring a ripple on the surface.
For about four years more we hear little in the
Diary concerning slavery. It was not until
1835, when the annexation of Texas began to be
mooted, that the North fairly took the alarm,
and the irrepressible conflict began to develop.
Then at once we find Mr. Adams at the front.
That he had always cherished an abhorrence of
slavery and a bitter antipathy to slave-holders
as a class is sufficiently indicated by many
chance remarks scattered through his Diary

from early years. Now that a great question,
vitally affecting the slave power, divided the
country into parties and inaugurated the struggle which never again slept until it was settled
forever by the result of the civil war, Mr. Adams at once assumed the function of leader.
His position should be clearly understood; for
in the vast labor which lay before the abolition
party different tasks fell to different men.   Mr.
Adams assumed to be neither an agitator nor a
reformer; by necessity of character, training,
fitness, and official position, he was a legislator
and statesman.   The task which accident or
destiny allotted to him was neither to preach
among the people a crusade against slavery, nor
to devise and keep in action the thousand resources which busy men throughout the country
were constantly multiplying for the purpose of
spreading and increasing a popular hostility
towards the great "institution."   Every great
cause has need of its fanatics, its vanguard to
keep far in advance of what is for the time
reasonable and possible; it has not less need
of the wiser and cooler heads to discipline and
control the great mass which is set in motion
by the reckless forerunners, to see to the ac-
complishment of that which the present circumstances and development of the movement allow
to be accomplished.   It fell to Mr. Adams to

direct the assault against the outworks which were then vulnerable, and to see that the force then possessed by the movement was put to such uses as would insure definite results instead of being wasted in endeavors which as yet were impossible of achievement. Drawing his duty from his situation and surroundings, he left to others, to younger men and more rhetorical natures, outside the walls of Congress, the business of firing the people and stirring popular opinion and sympathy. He was set to do that portion of the work of abolition which was to be done in Congress, to encounter the mighty efforts which were made to stifle the great humanitarian cry in the halls of the national legislature. This was quite as much as one man was equal to; in fact, it is certain that no one then in public life except Mr. Adams could have done it effectually. So obvious is this that one cannot help wondering what would have befallen the cause, had he not been just where he was to forward it in just the way that he did. It is only another among the many instances of the need surely finding the man. His qualifications were unique; his ability, his knowledge, his prestige and authority, his high personal character, his persistence and courage, his combativeness stimulated by an acrimonious temper but checked by a sound judgment, his

merciless power of invective, his independence
and carelessness of applause or vilification,
friendship or enmity, constituted him an opponent fully equal to the enormous odds which
the slave-holding interest arrayed against him.
A like moral and mental fitness was to be found
in no one else. Numbers could not overawe
him, nor loneliness dispirit him. He was
probably the most formidable fighter in debate
of whom parliamentary records preserve the
memory. The hostility which he encountered
beggars description; the English language was
deficient in adequate words of virulence and
contempt to express the feelings which were
entertained towards him. At home he had not
the countenance of that class in society to which
he naturally belonged. A second time he found
the chief part of the gentlemen of Boston and its
vicinity, the leading lawyers, the rich merchants,
the successful manufacturers, not only opposed
to him, but entertaining towards him sentiments
of personal dislike and even vindictiveness.
This stratum of the community, having a natural
distaste for disquieting agitation and influenced
by class feeling, — the gentlemen of the North
sympathizing with the " aristocracy " of the
South, — could not make common cause with
anti-slavery people. Fortunately, however, Mr.
Adams was returned by a country district where

the old Puritan instincts were still strong. The
intelligence and free spirit of New England were
at his back, and were fairly represented by him ;
in spite of high-bred disfavor they carried him
gallantly through the long struggle. The people
of the Plymouth district sent him back to the
House every two years from the time of his first
election to the year of his death, and the disgust
of the gentlemen of Boston was after all of
trifling consequence to him and of no serious
influence upon the course of history. The old
New England instinct was in him as it was in
the mass of the people ; that instinct made him
the real exponent of New England thought,
belief, and feeling, and that same instinct made
the great body of voters stand by him with
unswerving constancy. When his fellow Representatives, almost to a man, deserted him, he was
sustained by many a token of sympathy and admiration coming from among the people at large.
Time and the history of the United States have
been his potent vindicators. The conservative,
conscienceless respectability of wealth was, as
is usually the case with it in the annals of the
Anglo-Saxon race, quite in the wrong and predestined to well-merited defeat. It adds to the
honor due to Mr. Adams that his sense of right
was true enough, and that his vision was clear
enough, to lead him out of that strong thraldom

which class feelings, traditions, and comradeship
are wont to exercise.

But it is time to resume the narrative and to
let Mr. Adams's acts — of which after all it is
possible to give only the briefest sketch, select-
ing a few of the more striking incidents — tell
the tale of his Congressional life.

On February 14, 1835, Mr. Adams again presented two petitions for the abolition of slavery
in the District of Columbia, but without giving
rise to much excitement. The fusillade was,
however, getting too thick and fast to be en-
dured longer with indifference by the impatient
Southerners. At the next session of Congress
they concluded to try to stop it, and their ingenious scheme was to make Congress shot-
proof, so to speak, against such missiles. On
January 4, 1836, Mr. Adams presented an abolition petition couched in the usual form, and
moved that it be laid on the table, as others like
it had lately been. But in a moment Mr. Glas-
cock, of Georgia, moved that the petition be
not received. Debate sprang up on a point of
order, and two days later, before the question
of reception was determined, a resolution was
offered by Mr. Jarvis, of Maine, declaring that
the House would not entertain any petitions for
the abolition of slavery in the District of Columbia. This resolution was supported on the

ground that Congress had no constitutional
power in the premises. Some days later, January 18, 1836, before any final action had been
reached upon this proposition, Mr. Adams presented some more abolition petitions, one of
them signed by "one hundred and forty-eight
ladies, citizens of the Commonwealth of Massachusetts; for, I said, I had not yet brought myself to doubt whether females were citizens."
The usual motion not to receive was made, and
then a new device was resorted to in the shape
of a motion that the motion not to receive be
laid on the table.

On February 8, 1836, this novel scheme for
shutting off petitions against slavery immediately upon their presentation was referred to
a select committee of which Mr. Pinckney was
chairman. On May 18 this committee reported
in substance: 1. That Congress had no power
to interfere with slavery in any State; 2. That
Congress ought not to interfere with slavery in
the District of Columbia; 3. That whereas
the agitation of the subject was disquieting and
objectionable, "all petitions, memorials, resolutions or papers, relating in any way or to any
extent whatsoever to the subject of slavery or
the abolition of slavery, shall, without being
either printed or referred, be laid upon the
table, and that no further action whatever shall

be had thereon." When it came to taking a
vote upon this report a division of the question
was called for, and the yeas and nays were
ordered. The first resolution was then read,
whereupon Mr. Adams at once rose and pledged
himself, if the House would allow him five min-
utes' time, to prove it to be false. But cries of
" order " resounded; he was compelled to take
his seat and the resolution was adopted by 182
to 9. Upon the second resolution he asked to
be excused from voting, and his name was
passed in the call. The third resolution with
its preamble was then read, and Mr. Adams, so
soon as his name was called, rose and said : " I
hold the resolution to be a direct violation of
the Constitution of the United States, the rules
of this House, and the rights of my constituents." He was interrupted by shrieks of
" order " resounding on every side ; but he only
spoke the louder and obstinately finished his
sentence before resuming his seat. The resolution was of course agreed to, the vote standing
117 to 68. Such was the beginning of the famous " gag " which became and long remained
— afterward in a worse shape — a standing
rule of the House. Regularly in each new Congress when the adoption of rules came up, Mr.
Adams moved to rescind the " gag ; " but for
many years his motions continued to be voted

down, as a matter of course. Its imposition was clearly a mistake on the part of the slave-holding party; free debate would almost surely have hurt them less than this interference with the freedom of petition. They had assumed an untenable position. Henceforth, as the persistent advocate of the right of petition, Mr. Adams had a support among the people at large vastly greater than he could have enjoyed as the opponent of slavery. As his adversaries had shaped the issue he was predestined to victory in a free country.

A similar scene was enacted on December 21 and 22, 1837. A "gag" or "speech-smothering" resolution being then again before the House, Mr. Adams, when his name was called in the taking of the vote, cried out "amidst a perfect war-whoop of 'order:' 'I hold the resolution to be a violation of the Constitution, of the right of petition of my constituents and of the people of the United States, and of my right to freedom of speech as a member of this House.'" Afterward, in reading over the names of members who had voted, the clerk omitted that of Mr. Adams, this utterance of his not having constituted a vote. Mr. Adams called attention to the omission. The clerk, by direction of the Speaker, thereupon called his name. His only reply was by a motion that his answer as already made should be entered on the Journal. The Speaker said that this motion was not in order. Mr. Adams, resolute to get upon the record, requested that his motion with the Speaker's decision that it was not in order might be entered on the Journal. The next day, finding that this entry had not been made in proper shape, he brought up the matter again. One of his opponents made a false step, and Mr. Adams "bantered him" upon it until the other was provoked into saying that, "if the question ever came to the issue of war, the Southern people would march into New England and conquer it." Mr. Adams replied that no doubt they would if they could; that he entered his resolution upon the Journal because he was resolved that his opponent's "name should go down to posterity damned to everlasting fame." No one ever gained much in a war of words with this ever-ready and merciless tongue.

Mr. Adams, having soon become known to all the nation as the indomitable presenter of anti-slavery petitions, quickly found that great numbers of people were ready to keep him busy in this trying task. For a long while it was almost as much as he could accomplish to receive, sort, schedule, and present the infinite number of petitions and memorials which came to him praying for the abolition of slavery and of the

slave-trade in the District of Columbia, and opposing the annexation of Texas. It was an occupation not altogether devoid even of physical
danger, and calling for an amount of moral
courage greater than it is now easy to appreciate. It is the incipient stage of such a conflict that tests the mettle of the little band of
innovators. When it grows into a great party
question much less courage is demanded. The
mere presentation of an odious petition may
seem in itself to be a simple task; but to find
himself in a constant state of antagonism to a
powerful, active, and vindictive majority in a
debating body, constituted of such material as
then made up the House of Representatives,
wore hardly even upon the iron temper and inflexible disposition of Mr. Adams. "The most
insignificant error of conduct in me at this
time," he writes in April, 1837, "would be my
irredeemable ruin in this world; and both the
ruling political parties are watching with intense anxiety for some overt act by me to set
the whole pack of their hireling presses upon
me." But amid the host of foes, and aware
that he could count upon the aid of scarcely a
single hearty and daring friend, he labored only
the more earnestly. The severe pressure against
him begat only the more severe counter pressure
upon his part.

Besides these natural and legitimate difficulties, Mr. Adams was further in the embarrassing position of one who has to fear as much
from the imprudence of allies as from open hostility of antagonists, and he was often compelled
to guard against a peculiar risk coming from
his very coadjutors in the great cause.   The ex-
tremists who had cast aside all regard for what
was practicable, and who utterly scorned to consider the feasibility or the consequences of measures which seemed to them to be correct as abstract propositions of morality, were constantly
urging him to action which would only have
destroyed him forever in political life, would
have stripped him of his influence, exiled him
from that position in Congress where he could
render the most efficient service that was in
him, and left him naked of all usefulness and
utterly helpless to continue that essential portion of the labor which could be conducted by
no one else.   " The abolitionists generally," he
said, " are constantly urging me to indiscreet
movements, which would ruin me, and weaken
and not strengthen their cause."   His family,
on the other hand, sought to restrain him from
all connection with these dangerous partisans.
" Between these adverse impulses," he writes,
" my mind is agitated almost to distraction. . . .
I walk on the edge of a precipice almost every

step that I take." In the midst of all this anxiety, however, he was fortunately supported by the strong commendation of his constituents which they once loyally declared by formal and unanimous votes in a convention summoned for the express purpose of manifesting their support. His feelings appear by an entry in his Diary in October, 1837 : —

"I have gone [he said] as far upon this article, the abolition of slavery, as the public opinion of the free portion of the Union will bear, and so far that scarcely a slave-holding member of the House dares to vote with me upon any question. I have as yet been thoroughly sustained by my own State, but one step further and I hazard my own standing and influence there, my own final overthrow, and the cause of liberty itself for an indefinite time, certainly for more than my remnant of life. Were there in the House one member capable of taking the lead in this cause of universal emancipation, which is moving onward in the world and in this country, I would withdraw from the contest which will rage with increasing fury as it draws to its crisis, but for the management of which my age, infirmities, and approaching end totally disqualify me. There is no such man in the House."

September 15, 1837, he says : "I have been for some time occupied day and night, when at home, in assorting and recording the petitions

and remonstrances against the annexation of
Texas, and other anti-slavery petitions, which
flow upon me in torrents." The next day he
presented the singular petition of one Sherlock
S. Gregory, who had conceived the eccentric
notion of asking Congress to declare him "an
alien or stranger in the land so long as slavery
exists and the wrongs of the Indians are unre-
quited and unrepented of." September 28 he
presented a batch of his usual petitions, and
also asked leave to offer a resolution calling for
a report concerning the coasting trade in slaves.
"There was what Napoleon would have called
a superb NO! returned to my request from the
servile side of the House." The next day he
presented fifty-one more like documents, and
notes having previously presented one hundred
and fifty more.

In December, 1837, still at this same work,
he made a hard but fruitless effort to have the
Texan remonstrances and petitions sent to a
select committee instead of to that on foreign
affairs which was constituted in the Southern
interest. On December 29 he "presented several bundles of abolition and anti-slavery petitions," and said that, having declared his opinion that the gag-rule was unconstitutional, null,
and void, he should "submit to it only as to
physical force." January 3, 1838, he presented

" about a hundred petitions, memorials, and remonstrances, — all laid on the table." January
15 he presented fifty more. January 28 he received thirty-one petitions, and spent that day
and the next in assorting and filing these and
others which he previously had, amounting in
all to one hundred and twenty. February 14,
in the same year, was a field-day in the petition
campaign : he presented then no less than three
hundred and fifty petitions, all but three or four
of which bore more or less directly upon the
slavery question. Among these petitions was
one

"praying that Congress would take measures to
protect citizens from the North going to the South
from danger to their lives. When the motion to lay
that on the table was made, I said that, 'In another
part of the Capitol it had been threatened that if a
Northern abolitionist should go to North Carolina,
and utter a principle of the Declaration of Independence ' — Here a loud cry of ' order ! order ! ' burst
forth, in which the Speaker yelled the loudest. I
waited till it subsided, and then resumed, 'that if they
could catch him they would hang him ! ' I said this
so as to be distinctly heard throughout the hall, the
renewed deafening shout of ' order ! order ! ' notwithstanding. The Speaker then said, 'The gentleman
from Massachusetts will take his seat ; ' which I did
and immediately rose again and presented another
petition. He did not dare tell me that I could not

proceed without permission of the House, and I proceeded. The threat to hang Northern abolitionists
was uttered by Preston of the Senate within the last
fortnight."

On March 12, of the same year, he presented
ninety-six petitions, nearly all of an anti-slavery character, one of them for " expunging the
Declaration of Independence from the Jour-
nals."

On December 14, 1838, Mr. Wise, of Virginia, objected to the reception of certain anti-
slavery petitions. The Speaker ruled his objection out of order, and from this ruling Wise
appealed. The question on the appeal was
taken by yeas and nays. When Mr. Adams's
name was called, he relates : —

" I rose and said, ' Mr. Speaker, considering all the
resolutions introduced by the gentleman from New
Hampshire as ' — The Speaker roared out, ' The
gentleman from Massachusetts must answer Aye or
No, and nothing else. Order ! ' With a reinforced
voice — ' I refuse to answer, because I consider all
the proceedings of the House as unconstitutional ' —
While in a firm and swelling voice I pronounced distinctly these words, the Speaker and about two thirds
of the House cried, ' order ! order ! order ! ' till it became a perfect yell. I paused a moment for it to
cease and then said, ' a direct violation of the Constitution of the United States.' While speaking these

words with loud, distinct, and slow articulation, the
bawl of 'order! order!' resounded again from two
thirds of the House. The Speaker, with agonizing
lungs, screamed, 'I call upon the House to support
me in the execution of my duty!' I then coolly resumed my seat. Waddy Thompson, of South Carolina, advancing into one of the aisles with a sarcastic
smile and silvery tone of voice, said, 'What aid from
the House would the Speaker desire?' The Speaker
snarled back, 'The gentleman from South Carolina
is out of order!' and a peal of laughter burst forth
from all sides of the House."

So that little skirmish ended, much more
cheerfully than was often the case.

December 20, 1838, he presented fifty anti-
slavery petitions, among which were three praying for the recognition of the Republic of Hayti.
Petitions of this latter kind he strenuously insisted should be referred to a select committee,
or else to the Committee on Foreign Affairs,
accompanied in the latter case with explicit
instructions that a report thereon should be
brought in. He audaciously stated that he asked
for these instructions because so many petitions
of a like tenor had been sent to the Foreign
Affairs Committee, and had found it a limbo
from which they never again emerged, and the
chairman had said that this would continue to
be the case. The chairman, sitting two rows

behind Mr. Adams, said, "that insinuation should not be made against a gentleman!" "I shall make," retorted Mr. Adams, "what insinuation I please. This is not an insinuation, but a direct, positive assertion."

January 7, 1839, he cheerfully records that he presented ninety-five petitions, bearing "directly or indirectly upon the slavery topics," and some of them very exasperating in their language. March 30, 1840, he handed in no less than five hundred and eleven petitions, many of which were not receivable under the "gag" rule adopted on January 28 of that year, which had actually gone the length of refusing so much as a reception to abolition petitions. April 13, 1840, he presented a petition for the repeal of the laws in the District of Columbia, which authorized the whipping of women. Besides this he had a multitude of others, and he only got through the presentation of them "just as the morning hour expired." On January 21, 1841, he found much amusement in puzzling his Southern adversaries by presenting some petitions in which, besides the usual anti-slavery prayers, there was a prayer to refuse to admit to the Union any new State whose constitution should tolerate slavery. The Speaker said that only the latter prayer could be *received* under the "gag" rule. Connor, of

North Carolina, moved to lay on the table so much of the petition as could be received. Mr. Adams tauntingly suggested that in order to do this it would be necessary to mutilate the document by cutting it into two pieces ; whereat there was great wrath and confusion, " the House got into a snarl, the Speaker knew not what to do." The Southerners raved and fumed for a while, and finally resorted to their usual expedient, and dropped altogether a matter which so sorely burned their fingers.

A fact, very striking in view of the subsequent course of events, concerning Mr. Adams's relation with the slavery question, seems hitherto to have escaped the attention of those who have dealt with his career. It may as well find a place here as elsewhere in a narrative which it is difficult to make strictly chronological. Apparently he was the first to declare the doctrine, that the abolition of slavery could be lawfully accomplished by the exercise of the war powers of the Government. The earliest expression of this principle is found in a speech made by him in May, 1836, concerning the distribution of rations to fugitives from Indian hostilities in Alabama and Georgia. He then said : —

" From the instant that your slave-holding States become the theatre of war, civil, servile, or foreign,

from that instant the war powers of the Constitution
extend to interference with the institution of slavery
in every way in which it can be interfered with, from
a claim of indemnity for slaves taken or destroyed,
to a cession of the State burdened with slavery to a
foreign power."

In June, 1841, he made a speech of which no
report exists, but the contents of which may be
in part learned from the replies and references
to it which are on record. Therein he appears
to have declared that slavery could be abolished
in the exercise of the treaty-making power, having reference doubtless to a treaty concluding a
war.

These views were of course mere abstract expressions of opinion as to the constitutionality
of measures the real occurrence of which was
anticipated by nobody. But, as the first suggestions of a doctrine in itself most obnoxious
to the Southern theory and fundamentally de-
structive of the great Southern "institution"
under perfectly possible circumstances, this enun-
ciation by Mr. Adams gave rise to much indignation. Instead of allowing the imperfectly
formulated principle to lose its danger in oblivion, the Southerners assailed it with vehemence.
They taunted Mr. Adams with the opinion, as if
merely to say that he held it was to damn him
to everlasting infamy. The only result was that

they induced him to consider the matter more fully, and to express his belief more deliberately. In January, 1842, Mr. Wise attacked him upon this ground, and a month later Marshall followed in the same strain. These assaults were perhaps the direct incentive to what was said soon after by Mr. Adams, on April 14, 1842, in a speech concerning war with England and with Mexico, of which there was then some talk. Giddings, among other resolutions, had introduced one to the effect that the slave States had the exclusive right to be consulted on the subject of slavery. Mr. Adams said that he could not give his assent to this. One of the laws of war, he said, is

"that when a country is invaded, and two hostile armies are set in martial array, the commanders of both armies have power to emancipate all the slaves in the invaded territory."

He cited some precedents from South American history, and continued: —

"Whether the war be servile, civil, or foreign, I lay this down as the law of nations. I say that the military authority takes for the time the place of all municipal institutions, slavery among the rest. Under that state of things, so far from its being true that the States where slavery exists have the exclusive management of the subject, not only the President of the United States but the commander of the army has

power to order the universal emancipation of the
slaves."

This declaration of constitutional doctrine
was made with much positiveness and emphasis.
There for many years the matter rested. The
principle had been clearly asserted by Mr. Adams, angrily repudiated by the South, and in
the absence of the occasion of war there was
nothing more to be done in the matter. But
when the exigency at last came, and the government of the United States was brought face
to face with by far the gravest constitutional
problem presented by the great rebellion, then
no other solution presented itself save that which
had been suggested twenty years earlier in the
days of peace by Mr. Adams. It was in pur-
suance of the doctrine to which he thus gave
the first utterance that slavery was forever abolished in the United States. Extracts from the
last-quoted speech long stood as the motto of
the " Liberator ; " and at the time of the Emancipation Proclamation Mr. Adams was regarded
as the chief and sufficient authority for an act
so momentous in its effect, so infinitely useful
in a matter of national extremity. But it was
evidently a theory which had taken strong hold
upon him. Besides the foregoing speeches there
is an explicit statement of it in a letter which
he wrote from Washington April 4, 1836, to

Hon. Solomon Lincoln, of Hingham, a friend and constituent. After touching upon other topics he says : —

" The new pretensions of the slave representation in Congress of a right to refuse to receive petitions, and that Congress have no constitutional power to abolish slavery or the slave-trade in the District of Columbia, forced upon me so much of the discussion as I did take upon me, but in which you are well aware I did not and could not speak a tenth part of my mind. I did not, for example, start the question whether by the law of God and of nature man can hold *property*, HEREDITARY property, in man. I did not start the question whether in the event of a servile insurrection and war, Congress would not have complete unlimited control over the whole subject of slavery, even to the emancipation of all the slaves in the State where such insurrection should break out, and for the suppression of which the freemen of Plymouth and Norfolk counties, Massachusetts, should be called by Acts of Congress to pour out their treasures and to shed their blood. Had I spoken my mind on these two points, the sturdiest of the abolitionists would have disavowed the sentiments of their champion."

The projected annexation of Texas, which became a battle-ground whereon the tide of conflict swayed so long and so fiercely to and fro, profoundly stirred Mr. Adams's indignation. It is, he said, " a question of far deeper

root and more overshadowing branches than
any or all others that now agitate this country.
. . . I had opened it by my speech . . . on
the 25th May, 1836 — by far the most noted
speech that I ever made." He based his opposition to the annexation upon constitutional
objections, and on September 18, 1837, offered
a resolution that " the power of annexing the
people of any independent State to this Union
is a power not delegated by the Constitution of
the United States to their Congress or to any
department of their government, but reserved
to the people." The Speaker refused to receive the motion, or even allow it to be read,
on the ground that it was not in order. Mr.
Adams repeated substantially the same motion
in June, 1838, then adding "that any attempt
by act of Congress or by treaty to annex the
Republic of Texas to this Union would be an
usurpation of power which it would be the right
and the duty of the free people of the Union to
resist and annul." The story of his opposition
to this measure is, however, so interwoven with
his general antagonism to slavery, that there is
little occasion for treating them separately.[1]

[1] In an address to his constituents in September, 1842, Mr.
Adams spoke of his course concerning Texas. Having mentioned Mr. Van Buren's reply, declining the formal proposition
made in 1837 by the Republic of Texas for annexation to the
United States, he continued : " But the slave-breeding passion

People sometimes took advantage of his
avowed principles concerning freedom of petition to put him in positions which they thought
would embarrass him or render him ridiculous.
Not much success, however, attended these foolish efforts of shallow wits. It was not easy to
disconcert him or to take him at disadvantage.
July 28, 1841, he presented a paper of this
character coming from sundry Virginians and
praying that all the free colored population
should be sold or expelled from the country.
He simply stated as he handed in the sheet that

for the annexation was not to be so disconcerted. At the en-
suing session of Congress numerous petitions and memorials
for and against the annexation were presented to the House,
. . . and were referred to the Committee of Foreign Affairs,
who, without ever taking them into consideration, towards the
close of the session asked to be discharged from the consideration of them all. It was on this report that the debate arose,
in which I disclosed the whole system of duplicity and perfidy
towards Mexico, which had marked the Jackson Administration from its commencement to its close. It silenced the
clamors for the annexation of Texas to this Union for three
years till the catastrophe of the Van Buren Administration.
The people of the free States were lulled into the belief that
the whole project was abandoned, and that they should hear
no more of slave-trade cravings for the annexation of Texas
Had Harrison lived they would have heard no more of them
to this day, but no sooner was John Tyler installed in the
President's House than nullification and Texas and war with
Mexico rose again upon the surface, with eye steadily fixed
upon the Polar Star of Southern slave-dealing supremacy in
the government of the Union."

nothing could be more abhorrent to him than this prayer, and that his respect for the right of petition was his only motive for presenting this. It was suspended under the " gag " rule, and its promoters, unless very easily amused, must have been sadly disappointed with the fate and effect of their joke. On March 5, 1838, he received from Rocky Mount in Virginia a letter and petition praying that the House would arraign at its bar and forever expel John Quincy Adams. He presented both documents, with a resolution asking that they be referred to a committee for investigation and report. His enemies in the House saw that he was sure to have the best of the sport if the matter should be pursued, and succeeded in laying it on the table. Waddy Thompson thoughtfully improved the opportunity to mention to Mr. Adams that he also had received a petition, " numerously signed," praying for Mr. Adams's expulsion, but had never presented it. In the following May Mr. Adams presented another petition of like tenor. Dromgoole said that he supposed it was a " quiz," and that he would move to lay it on the table, " unless the gentleman from Massachusetts wished to give it another direction." Mr. Adams said that " the gentleman from Massachusetts cared very little about it," and it found the limbo of the " table."

To this same period belongs the memorable
tale of Mr. Adams's attempt to present a petition from slaves. On February 6, 1837, he
brought in some two hundred abolition petitions. He closed with one against the slave-
trade in the District of Columbia purporting
to be signed by "nine ladies of Fredericksburg,
Virginia," whom he declined to name because,
as he said, in the present disposition of the
country, "he did not know what might happen
to them if he did name them." Indeed, he
added, he was not sure that the petition was
genuine ; he had said, when he began to present his petitions, that some among them were
so peculiar that he was in doubt as to their
genuineness, and this fell within the description. Apparently he had concluded and was
about to take his seat, when he quickly caught
up another sheet, and said that he held in his
hand a paper concerning which he should wish
to have the decision of the Speaker before presenting it. It purported to be a petition from
twenty-two slaves, and he would like to know
whether it came within the rule of the House
concerning petitions relating to slavery. The
Speaker, in manifest confusion, said that he
could not answer the question until he knew
the contents of the document. Mr. Adams,
remarking that " it was one of those petitions

which had occurred to his mind as not being
what it purported to be," proposed to send it
up to the Chair for inspection. Objection was
made to this, and the Speaker said that the
circumstances were so extraordinary that he
would take the sense of the House. That body,
at first inattentive, now became interested, and
no sooner did a knowledge of what was going
on spread among those present than great
excitement prevailed. Members were hastily
brought in from the lobbies ; many tried to
speak, and from parts of the hall cries of
" Expel him ! Expel him ! " were heard. For
a brief interval no one of the enraged Southerners was equal to the unforeseen emergency.
Mr. Haynes moved the rejection of the petition.   Mr. Lewis deprecated this motion, being
of opinion that the House must inflict punishment on the gentleman from Massachusetts.
Mr. Haynes thereupon withdrew a motion which
was so obviously inadequate to the vindictive
gravity of the occasion.   Mr. Grantland stood
ready to second a motion to punish Mr. Adams,
and Mr. Lewis said that if punishment should
not be meted out it would " be better for the
representatives from the slave-holding States to
go home at once."   Mr. Alford said that so
soon as the petition should be presented he
would move that it should " be taken from the

House and burned." At last Mr. Thompson
got a resolution into shape as follows : —

"That the Hon. John Quincy Adams, by the attempt just made by him to introduce a petition purporting on its face to be from slaves, has been guilty
of a gross disrespect to this House, and that he be
instantly brought to the bar to receive the severe
censure of the Speaker."

In supporting this resolution he said that
Mr. Adams's action was in gross and wilful violation of the rules of the House and an insult
to its members. He even threatened criminal
proceedings before the grand jury of the District of Columbia, saying that if that body had
the " proper intelligence and spirit " people
might " yet see an incendiary brought to con-
dign punishment." Mr. Haynes, not satisfied
with Mr. Thompson's resolution, proposed a
substitute to the effect that Mr. Adams had
" rendered himself justly liable to the severest
censure of this House and is censured accordingly." Then there ensued a little more excited
speech-making and another resolution, that Mr.
Adams,

" by his attempt to introduce into this House a
petition from slaves for the abolition of slavery in
the District of Columbia, has committed an outrage
on the feelings of the people of a large portion of this

Union ; a flagrant contempt on the dignity of this
House ; and, by extending to slaves a privilege only
belonging to freemen, directly incites the slave population to insurrection ; and that the said member be
forthwith called to the bar of the House and be cen·
sured by the Speaker."

Mr. Lewis remained of opinion that it might
be best for the Southern members to go home,
— a proposition which afterwards drew forth a
flaming speech from Mr. Alford, who, far from
inclining to go home, was ready to stay " until
this fair city is a field of Waterloo and this
beautiful Potomac a river of blood." Mr.
Patton, of Virginia, was the first to speak a
few words to bring members to their senses,
pertinently asking whether Mr. Adams had
" attempted to offer " this petition, and whether
it did indeed pray for the abolition of slavery.
It might be well, he suggested, for his friends
to be sure of their facts before going further.
Then at last Mr. Adams, who had not at all
lost his head in the general hurly-burly, rose
and said, that amid these numerous resolutions
charging him with " high crimes and misde-
meanors " and calling him to the bar of the
House to answer for the same, he had thought it
proper to remain silent until the House should
take some action ; that he did not suppose
that, if he should be brought to the bar of the

House, he should be "struck mute by the previous question" before he should have been given an opportunity to "say a word or two" in his own defence. As to the facts : "I did not present the petition," he said, "and I appeal to the Speaker to say that I did not. . . . I intended to take the decision of the Speaker before I went one step towards presenting or offering to present that petition." The contents of the petition, should the House ever choose to read it, he continued, would render necessary some amendments at least in the last resolution, since the prayer was that slavery should *not* be abolished ! "The gentleman from Alabama may perchance find, that the object of this petition is precisely what he desires to accomplish ; and that these slaves who have sent this paper to me are his auxiliaries instead of being his opponents."

These remarks caused some discomfiture among the Southern members, who were glad to have time for deliberation given them by a maundering speech from Mr. Mann, of New York, who talked about "the deplorable spectacle shown off every petition day by the honorable member from Massachusetts in presenting the abolition petitions of his infatuated friends and constituents," charged Mr. Adams with running counter to the sense of the whole

country with a "violence paralleled only by
the revolutionary madness of desperation," and
twitted him with his political friendlessness,
with his age, and with the insinuation of wan-
ing faculties and judgment. This little phial
having been emptied, Mr. Thompson arose and
angrily assailed Mr. Adams for contemptuously
trifling with the House, which charge he based
upon the entirely unproved assumption that
the petition was not a genuine document. He
concluded by presenting new resolutions better adapted to the recent development of the
case : —

"1. That the Hon. John Quincy Adams, by an
effort to present a petition from slaves, has committed
a gross contempt of this House.

"2. That the member from Massachusetts above-
named, by creating the impression and leaving the
House under such impression, that the said petition
was for the abolition of slavery, when he knew that
it was not, has trifled with the House.

"3. That the Hon. John Quincy Adams receive the
censure of the House for his conduct referred to in
the preceding resolutions."

Mr. Pinckney said that the avowal by Mr.
Adams that he had in his possession the petition of slaves was an admission of communication with slaves, and so was evidence of col-
lusion with them ; and that Mr. Adams had

thus rendered himself indictable for aiding and abetting insurrection. *A fortiori*, then, was he not amenable to the censure of the House? Mr. Haynes, of Georgia, forgetting that the petition had not been presented, announced his intention of moving that it should be rejected subject only to a permission for its withdrawal; another member suggested that, if the petition should be disposed of by burning, it would be well to commit to the same combustion the gentleman who presented it.

On the next day some more resolutions were ready, prepared by Dromgoole, who in his sober hours was regarded as the best parliamentarian in the Southern party. These were, that Mr. Adams

"by stating in his place that he had in his possession a paper purporting to be a petition from slaves, and inquiring if it came within the meaning of a resolution heretofore adopted (as preliminary to its presentation), has given color to the idea that slaves have the right of petition and of his readiness to be their organ; and that for the same he deserves the censure of the House.

"That the aforesaid John Quincy Adams receive a censure from the Speaker in the presence of the House of Representatives."

Mr. Alford, in advocating these resolutions, talked about " this awful crisis of our beloved

country." Mr. Robertson, though opposing
the resolutions, took pains "strongly to condemn . . . the conduct of the gentleman from
Massachusetts." Mr. Adams's colleague, Mr.
Lincoln, spoke in his behalf, so also did Mr.
Evans, of Maine; and Caleb Cushing made a
powerful speech upon his side. Otherwise than
this Mr. Adams was left to carry on the contest single-handed against the numerous array
of assailants, all incensed and many fairly sav-
age. Yet it is a striking proof of the dread
in which even the united body of hot-blooded
Southerners stood of this hard fighter from the
North, that as the debate was drawing to a close,
after they had all said their say and just before
his opportunity came for making his elaborate speech of defence, they suddenly and op-
portunely became ready to content themselves
with a mild resolution, which condemned generally the presentation of petitions from slaves,
and, for the disposal of this particular case,
recited that Mr. Adams had "solemnly dis-
claimed all design of doing anything disrespect-
ful to the House," and had "avowed his intention not to offer to present" to the House the
petition of this kind held by him; that "therefore all further proceedings in regard to his
conduct do now cease." A sneaking effort by
Mr. Vanderpoel to close Mr. Adams's mouth

by moving the previous question involved too much cowardice to be carried; and so on February 9 the sorely bated man was at last able to begin his final speech. He conducted his defence with singular spirit and ability, but at too great length to admit of even a sketch of what he said. He claimed the right of petition for slaves, and established it so far as argument can establish anything. He alleged that all he had done was to ask a question of the Speaker, and if he was to be censured for so doing, then how much more, he asked, was the Speaker deserving of censure who had even put the same question to the House, and given as his reason for so doing that it was not only of novel but of difficult import! He repudiated the idea that any member of the House could be held by a grand jury to respond for words spoken in debate, and recommended the gentlemen who had indulged in such preposterous threats "to study a little the first principles of civil liberty," excoriating them until they actually arose and tried to explain away their own language. He cast infinite ridicule upon the unhappy expression of Dromgoole, "giving color to an idea." Referring to the difficulty which he encountered by reason of the variety and disorder of the resolutions and charges against him with which "gentlemen from the South

had pounced down upon him like so many
eagles upon a dove," — there was an exquisite
sarcasm in the simile ! — he said : " When I
take up one idea, before I can give color to
the idea, it has already changed its form and
presents itself for consideration under other
colors. . . . What defence can be made against
this new crime of giving color to ideas ? " As
for trifling with the House by presenting a
petition which in the course of debate had become pretty well known and acknowledged to
be a hoax designed to lead Mr. Adams into a
position of embarrassment and danger, he dis-
claimed any such motive, reminding members
that he had given warning, when beginning to
present his petitions, that he was suspicious
that some among them might not be genuine.[1]
But while denying all intention of trifling with

[1] Mr. Adams afterward said : " I believed the petition signed
by female names to be genuine. . . . I had suspicions that the
other, purporting to be from slaves, came really from the hand
of a master who had prevailed on his slaves to sign it, that
they might have the appearance of imploring the members
from the North to cease offering petitions for their emancipation, which could have no other tendency than to aggravate
their servitude, and of being so impatient under the operation
of petitions in their favor as to pray that the Northern members who should persist in presenting them should be expelled." It was a part of the prayer of the petition that Mr.
Adams should be expelled if he should continue to present
abolition petitions.

the House, he rejected the mercy extended to him in the last of the long series of resolutions before that body. " I disclaim not," he said, " any particle of what I have done, not a single word of what I have said do I unsay ; nay, I am ready to do and to say the same to-morrow." He had no notion of aiding in making a loophole through which his blundering enemies might escape, even though he himself should be accorded the privilege of crawling through it with them. At times during his speech " there was great agitation in the House," but when he closed no one seemed ambitious to reply. His enemies had learned anew a lesson, often taught to them before and often to be impressed upon them again, that it was perilous to come to close quarters with Mr. Adams. They gave up all idea of censuring him, and were content to apply a very mild emollient to their own smarting wounds in the shape of a resolution, to the effect that slaves did not possess the right of petition secured by the Constitution to the people of the United States.

In the winter of 1842–43 the questions arising out of the affair of the Creole rendered the position then held by Mr. Adams at the head of the House Committee on Foreign Affairs exceedingly distasteful to the slave-holders. On

January 21, 1842, a somewhat singular manifestation of this feeling was made when Mr.
Adams himself presented a petition from Georgia praying for his removal from this Chairmanship. Upon this he requested to be heard
in his own behalf. The Southern party, not
sanguine of any advantage from debating the
matter, tried to lay it on the table. The petition was alleged by Habersham, of Georgia, to
be undoubtedly another hoax. But Mr. Adams,
loath to lose a good opportunity, still claimed
to be heard on the charges made against him
by the "infamous slave-holders." Mr. Smith, of
Virginia, said that the House had lately given
Mr. Adams leave to defend himself against the
charge of monomania, and asked whether he
was doing so. Some members cried "Yes!
Yes!"; others shouted "No! he is establishing
the fact." The wrangling was at last brought
to an end by the Speaker's declaration, that the
petition must lie over for the present. But the
scene had been only the prelude to one much
longer, fiercer, and more exciting. No sooner
was the document thus temporarily disposed of
than Mr. Adams rose and presented the petition of forty-five citizens of Haverhill, Massachusetts, praying the House "immediately to
adopt measures peaceably to dissolve the union
of these States," for the alleged cause of the

incompatibility between free and slave-holding communities. He moved " its reference to a select committee, with instructions to report an answer to the petitioners showing the reasons why the prayer of it ought not to be granted."

In a moment the House was aflame with excitement. The numerous members who hated Mr. Adams thought that at last he was experiencing the divinely sent madness which fore-runs destruction. Those who sought his political annihilation felt that the appointed and glorious hour of extinction had come : those who had writhed beneath the castigation of his invective exulted in the near revenge. While one said that the petition should never have been brought within the walls of the House, and another wished to burn it in the presence of the members, Mr. Gilmer, of Virginia, offered a resolution, that in presenting the petition Mr. Adams " had justly incurred the censure of the House." Some objection was made to this resolution as not being in order ; but Mr. Adams said that he hoped that it would be received and debated and that an opportunity would be given him to speak in his own defence ; " especially as the gentleman from Virginia had thought proper to play second fiddle to his colleague [1] from Accomac." Mr. Gilmer

[1] Henry A. Wise.

retorted that he "played second fiddle to no
man. He was no fiddler, but was endeavoring
to prevent the music of him who,

> 'In the space of one revolving moon,
> Was statesman, poet, fiddler, and buffoon.'"

The resolution was then laid on the table. The
House rose, and Mr. Adams went home and
noted in his Diary, "evening in meditation,"
for which indeed he had abundant cause. On
the following day Thomas F. Marshall, of Kentucky, offered a substitute for Gilmer's resolution. This new fulmination had been prepared
in a caucus of forty members of the slave-holding party, and was long and carefully framed.
Its preamble recited, in substance, that a petition to dissolve the Union, proposing to Congress
to destroy that which the several members had
solemnly and officially sworn to support, was a
"high breach of privilege, a contempt offered to
this House, a direct proposition to the Legislature and each member of it to commit perjury,
and involving necessarily in its execution and
its consequences the destruction of our country
and the crime of high treason:" wherefore it
was to be resolved that Mr. Adams, in presenting a petition for dissolution, had "offered the
deepest indignity to the House" and "an insult
to the people;" that if "this outrage" should
be "permitted to pass unrebuked and unpun-

ished " he would have " disgraced his country
. . . in the eyes of the whole world ; " that for
this insult and this " wound at the Constitution
and existence of his country, the peace, the se-
curity and liberty of the people of these States "
he " might well be held to merit expulsion from
the national councils ; " and that " the House
deem it an act of grace and mercy when they
only inflict upon him their severest censure ; "
that so much they must do " for the maintenance
of their own purity and dignity ; for the rest
they turned him over to his own conscience and
the indignation of all true American citizens."

These resolutions were then advocated by
Mr. Marshall at great length and with extreme
bitterness. Mr. Adams replied shortly, stating
that he should wish to make his full defence at
a later stage of the debate. Mr. Wise followed
in a personal and acrimonious harangue ; Mr.
Everett [1] gave some little assistance to Mr.
Adams, and the House again adjourned. The
following day Wise continued his speech, very
elaborately. When he closed, Mr. Adams, who
had " determined not to interrupt him till he
had discharged his full cargo of filthy invective," rose to " make a preliminary point." He
questioned the right of the House to entertain
Marshall's resolutions since the preamble as-

[1] Horace Everett, of Vermont.

sumed him to be guilty of the crimes of subornation of perjury and treason, and the resolutions themselves censured him as if he had been found guilty; whereas in fact he had not been tried upon these charges and of course had not been convicted. If he was to be brought to trial upon them he asserted his right to have the proceedings conducted before a jury of his peers, and that the House was not a tribunal having this authority. But if he was to be tried for contempt, for which alone he could lawfully be tried by the House, still there were an hundred members sitting on its benches who were morally disqualified to judge him, who could not give him an impartial trial, because they were prejudiced and the question was one "on which their personal, pecuniary, and most sordid interests were at stake." Such considerations, he said, ought to prevent many gentlemen from voting, as Mr. Wise had avowed that they would prevent him. Here Wise interrupted to disavow that he was influenced by any such reasons, but rather, he said, by the "personal loathing, dread, and contempt I feel for the man." Mr. Adams, continuing after this pleasant interjection, admitted that he was in the power of the majority, who might try him against law and condemn him against right if they would.

"If they say they will try me, they must try me. If they say they will punish me, they must punish me. But if they say that in peace and mercy they will spare me expulsion, I disdain and cast away their mercy; and I ask them if they will come to such a trial and expel me. I defy them. I have constituents to go to who will have something to say if this House expels me. Nor will it be long before the gentlemen will see me here again."

Such was the fierce temper and indomitable courage of this inflexible old man! He flung contempt in the face of those who had him wholly in their power, and in the same breath in which he acknowledged that power he dared them to use it. He charged Wise with the guilt of innocent blood, in connection with certain transactions in a duel, and exasperated that gentleman into crying out that the "charge made by the gentleman from Massachusetts was as base and black a lie as the traitor was base and black who uttered it." When he was asked by the Speaker to put his point of order in writing, — his own request to the like effect in another case having been refused shortly before, — he tauntingly congratulated that gentleman "upon his discovery of the expediency of having points of order reduced to writing — a favor which he had repeatedly denied to me." When Mr. Wise was speaking, "I interrupted him oc-

casionally," says Mr. Adams, "sometimes to
provoke him into absurdity." As usual he was
left to fight out his desperate battle substantially single-handed. Only Mr. Everett occasionally helped him a very little ; while one or
two others who spoke against the resolutions
were careful to explain that they felt no personal good will towards Mr. Adams. But he
faced the odds courageously. It was no new
thing for him to be pitted alone against a " solid
South." Outside the walls of the House he had
some sympathy and some assistance tendered
him by individuals, among others by Rufus
Choate then in the Senate, and by his own colleagues from Massachusetts. This support aided
and cheered him somewhat, but could not prevent substantially the whole burden of the labor
and brunt of the contest from bearing upon him
alone. Among the external manifestations of
feeling, those of hostility were naturally largely
in the ascendant. The newspapers of Washington — the " Globe " and the " National Intelligencer " — which reported the debates, daily filled
their columns with all the abuse and invective
which was poured forth against him, while they
gave the most meagre statements, or none at
all, of what he said in his own defence. Among
other amenities he received from North Carolina
an anonymous letter threatening him with assas-

sination, having also an engraved portrait of him with the mark of a rifle-ball in the forehead, and the motto "to stop the music of John Quincy Adams," etc., etc. This missive he read and displayed in the House, but it was received with profound indifference by men who would not have greatly objected to the execution of the barbarous threat.

The prolonged struggle cost him deep anxiety and sleepless nights, which in the declining years of a laborious life told hardly upon his aged frame. But against all odds of numbers and under all disadvantages of circumstances the past repeated itself, and Mr. Adams alone won a victory over all the cohorts of the South. Several attempts had been made during the debate to lay the whole subject on the table. Mr. Adams said that he would consent to this simply because his defence would be a very long affair, and he did not wish to have the time of the House consumed and the business of the nation brought to a stand solely for the consideration of his personal affairs. These propositions failing, he began his speech and soon was making such headway that even his adversaries were constrained to see that the opportunity which they had conceived to be within their grasp was eluding them, as had so often happened before. Accordingly on February 7 the

motion to " lay the whole subject on the table
forever " was renewed and carried by one hundred and six votes to ninety-three.   The House
then took up the original petition and refused
to receive it by one hundred and sixty-six to
forty.   No sooner was this consummation reached
than the irrepressible champion rose to his feet
and proceeded with his budget of anti-slavery
petitions, of which he " presented nearly two
hundred, till the House adjourned."

Within a very short time there came further
and convincing proof that Mr. Adams was vic-
tor.   On February 26 he writes : " D. D. Barnard told me he had received a petition from
his District, signed by a small number of very
respectable persons, praying for a dissolution of
the Union.   He said he did not know what to
do with it.   I dined with him."   By March 14
this dinner bore fruit.   Mr. Barnard had made
up his mind " what to do with it."   He presented it, with a motion that it be referred to a
select committee with instructions to report ad-
versely to its prayer.   The well-schooled House
now took the presentation without a ripple of
excitement, and was content with simply voting
not to receive the petition.

In the midst of the toil and anxiety imposed
upon Mr. Adams by this effort to censure and
disgrace him, the scheme, already referred to,

for displacing him from the chairmanship of the
Committee on Foreign Affairs had been actively
prosecuted.   He was notified that the Southern
members had formed a cabal for removing him
and putting Caleb Cushing in his place.   The
plan was, however, temporarily checked, and so
soon as Mr. Adams had triumphed in the House
the four Southern members of the committee
sent to the House a paper begging to be excused
from further services on the committee, " because
from recent occurrences it was doubtful whether
the House would remove the chairman, and they
were unwilling to serve with one in whom they
had no confidence."   The fugitives were granted,
" by a shout of acclamation," the excuse which
they sought for so welcome a reason, and the
same was also done for a fifth member.   Three
more of the same party, nominated to fill these
vacancies, likewise asked to be excused, and were
so.   Their letters preferring this request were
" so insulting personally " to Mr. Adams as to
constitute " gross breaches of privilege."   " The
Speaker would have refused to receive or present
them had they referred to any other man in the
House."   They were published, but Mr. Adams,
after some hesitation, determined not to give
them the importance which would result from
any public notice in the House upon his part.
He could afford to keep silence, and judged
wisely in doing so.

Amid all the animosity and rancor entertained towards Mr. Adams, there yet lurked
a degree of respect for his courage, honesty,
and ability which showed itself upon occasion,
doubtless not a little to the surprise of the
members themselves who were hardly conscious
that they entertained such sentiments until
startled into a manifestation of them. An eminent instance of this is to be found in the story
of the troubled days preceding the organization
of the twenty-sixth Congress. On December
2, 1839, the members elect of that body came
together in Washington, with the knowledge
that the seats of five gentlemen from New Jersey, who brought with them the regular guber-
natorial certificate of their election, would be
contested by five other claimants. According
to custom Garland, clerk of the last House,
called the assemblage to order and began the
roll-call. When he came to New Jersey he
called the name of one member from that State,
and then said that there were five other seats
which were contested, and that not feeling
authorized to decide the dispute he would pass
over the names of the New Jersey members
and proceed with the roll till the House should
be formed, when the question could be decided.
Plausible as appeared this abstention from an
exercise of authority in so grave a dispute, it

was nevertheless really an assumption and not a deprecation of power, and as such was altogether unjustifiable. The clerk's sole business was to call the names of those persons who presented the usual formal credentials; he had no right to take cognizance that the seats of any such persons might be the subject of a contest, which could properly be instituted, conducted, and determined only before and by the House itself when organized. But his course was not innocent of a purpose. So evenly was the House divided that the admission or exclusion of these five members in the first instance would determine the political complexion of the body. The members holding the certificates were Whigs; if the clerk could keep them out until the organization of the House should be completed, then the Democrats would control that organization, would elect their Speaker, and through him would make up the committees.

Naturally enough this arrogation of power by the clerk, the motives and consequences of which were abundantly obvious, raised a terrible storm. The debate continued till four o'clock in the afternoon, when a motion was made to adjourn. The clerk said that he could put no question, not even of adjournment, till the House should be formed. But there was a general cry to adjourn, and the clerk declared the House

adjourned.   Mr. Adams went home and wrote
in his Diary that the clerk's "two decisions form
together an insurmountable objection to the
transaction of any business, and an impossibility
of organizing the House. . . . The most curious
part of the case is, that his own election as clerk
depends upon the exclusion of the New Jersey
members." The next day was consumed in a
fierce debate as to whether the clerk should be
allowed to read an explanatory statement. Again
the clerk refused to put the question of adjournment, but, "upon inspection," declared an adjournment. Some called out "a count! a count!"
while most rushed out of the hall, and Wise
cried loudly, "Now we are a mob!" The next
day there was more violent debating, but no
progress towards a decision. Various party
leaders offered resolutions, none of which accomplished anything. The condition was ridiculous, disgraceful, and not without serious possibilities of danger. Neither did any light of
encouragement break in any quarter. In the
crisis there seemed, by sudden consent of all, to
be a turning towards Mr. Adams. Prominent
men of both parties came to him and begged
him to interfere. He was reluctant to plunge
into the embroilment; but the great urgency
and the abundant assurances of support placed
little less than actual compulsion upon him.

Henry A. Wise

Henry A Wise

Accordingly on December 5 he rose to address
the House. He was greeted as a *Deus ex
machina.* Not speaking to the clerk, but turning directly to the assembled members, he began: " Fellow citizens! Members elect of the
twenty-sixth Congress!" He could not resist
the temptation of administering a brief but severe and righteous castigation to Garland; and
then, ignoring that functionary altogether, proceeded to beg the House to *organize itself.* To
this end he said that he would offer a resolution
" ordering the clerk to call the members from
New Jersey possessing the credentials from the
Governor of that State." There had been already no lack of resolutions, but the difficulty
lay in the clerk's obstinate refusal to put the
question upon them. So now the puzzled cry
went up: "How shall the question be put?"
" I intend to put the question myself," said the
dauntless old man, wholly equal to the emergency. A tumult of applause resounded upon
all sides. Rhett, of South Carolina, sprang up
and offered a resolution, that Williams, of North
Carolina, the oldest member of the House, be
appointed chairman of the meeting; but upon
objection by Williams, he substituted the name
of Mr. Adams, and put the question. He was
" answered by an almost universal shout in the
affirmative." Whereupon Rhett and Williams

conducted the old man to the chair. It was
a proud moment. Wise, of Virginia, afterward
said, addressing a complimentary speech to Mr.
Adams, "and if, when you shall be gathered to
your fathers, I were asked to select the words
which in my judgment are calculated to give at
once the best character of the man, I would in-
scribe upon your tomb this sentence, 'I will put
the question myself!'" Doubtless Wise and a
good many more would have been glad enough
to put almost any epitaph on a tombstone for
Mr. Adams.[1] It must, however, be acknowledged that the impetuous Southerners behaved
very handsomely by their arch foe on this occasion, and were for once as chivalrous in fact as
they always were in profession.

Smooth water had by no means been reached
when Mr. Adams was placed at the helm ; on
the contrary, the buffeting became only the
more severe when the members were no longer
restrained by a lurking dread of grave disaster
if not of utter shipwreck. Between two bitterly
incensed and evenly divided parties engaged in
a struggle for an important prize, Mr. Adams,
having no strictly lawful authority pertaining

[1] Not quite two years later, pending a motion to reprimand
Mr. Wise for fighting with a member on the floor of the
House, that gentleman took pains insultingly to say, "that
there was but one man in the House whose judgment he was
unwilling to abide by," and that man was Mr. Adams.

to his singular and anomalous position, was hard
taxed to perform his functions. It is impossible to follow the intricate and acrimonious
quarrels of the eleven days which succeeded
until on December 16, upon the eleventh ballot,
R. M. T. Hunter, of Virginia, was elected
Speaker, and Mr. Adams was relieved from the
most arduous duty imposed upon him during his
life. In the course of the debates there had
been " much vituperation and much equally
unacceptable compliment " lavished upon him.
After the organization of the House, there was
some talk of moving a vote of thanks, but he
entreated that it should not be done. " In the
rancorous and bitter temper of the Administration party, exasperated by their disappointment
in losing their Speaker, the resolution of thanks,"
he said, "would have been lost if it had been
offered." However this might have been, history has determined this occurrence to have
been one of the most brilliant episodes in a life
which had many distinctions.

A few incidents indicative of respect must
have been welcome enough in the solitary fight-
laden career of Mr. Adams. He needed some
occasional encouragement to keep him from
sinking into despondency ; for though he was of
so unyielding and belligerent a disposition, of
such ungracious demeanor, so uncompromising

with friend and foe, yet he was a man of deep
and strong feelings, and in a way even very
sensitive though a proud reserve kept the secret
of this quality so close that few suspected it.
His Diary during his Congressional life shows a
man doing his duty sternly rather than cheerfully, treading resolutely a painful path, having
the reward which attends upon a clear conscience,
but neither light-hearted nor often even happy.
Especially he was frequently disappointed at the
returns which he received from others, and considered himself " ill-treated by every public man
whom circumstances had brought into competi-
tion with him ; " they had returned his " acts of
kindness and services " with " gross injustice."
The reflection did not induce him to deflect his
course in the least, but it was made with much
bitterness of spirit. Toward the close of 1835
he writes : —

" Among the dark spots in human nature which in
the course of my life I have observed, the devices of
rivals to ruin me have been sorry pictures of the
heart of man. . . . H. G. Otis, Theophilus Parsons,
Timothy Pickering, James A. Bayard, Henry Clay,
Jonathan Russell, William H. Crawford, John C.
Calhoun, Andrew Jackson, Daniel Webster, and John
Davis, W. B. Giles, and John Randolph, have used
up their faculties in base and dirty tricks to thwart
my progress in life and destroy my character."

Truly a long and exhaustive list of enmities! One can but suspect that a man of so many quarrels must have been quarrelsome. Certain it is, however, that in nearly every difference which Mr. Adams had in his life a question of right and wrong, of moral or political principle, had presented itself to him. His intention was always good, though his manner was so habitually irritating. He himself says that to nearly all these men — Russell alone specifically excepted — he had " returned good for evil," that he had " never wronged any one of them," and had even " neglected too much his self-defence against them." In October, 1833, he said : " I subject myself to so much toil and so much enmity, with so very little apparent fruit, that I sometimes ask myself whether I do not mistake my own motives. The best actions of my life make me nothing but enemies." In February, 1841, he made a powerful speech in castigation of Henry A. Wise, who had been upholding in Southern fashion slavery, duelling, and nullification. He received afterward some messages of praise and sympathy, but noted with pain that his colleagues thought it one of his " eccentric, wild, extravagant freaks of passion ; " and with a pathetic sense of loneliness he adds : " All around me is cold and discouraging and my own feelings are wound up to a pitch that my reason can scarcely endure." A few days later he had the pleasure of hearing one of the members say, in a speech, that there was an opinion among many that Mr. Adams was insane and did not know what he said. While a fight was going on such incidents only fired his blood, but afterwards the reminiscence affected his spirits cruelly.

In August, 1840, he writes that he has been twelve years submitting in silence to the "foulest and basest aspersions," to which it would have been waste of time to make reply, since the public ear had not been open to him. "Is the time arriving," he asks, "for me to speak? or must I go down to the grave and leave posterity to do justice to my father and to me?"

He has had at least the advantage of saying his say to posterity in a very effective and convincing shape in that Diary, which so discomfited and enraged General Jackson. There is plain enough speaking in its pages, which were a safety valve whereby much wrath escaped. Mr. Adams had the faculty of forcible expression when he chose to employ it, as may be seen from a few specimen sentences. On March 28, 1840, he remarks that Atherton "this day emitted half an hour of his rotten breath against" a pending bill. Atherton was infamous as the mover of the "gag" resolution, and Mr. Adams abhorred him accordingly. Duncan, of Cincinnati, mentioned as " delivering a dose of balderdash," is described as " the prime bully of the Kinderhook Democracy," without " perception of any moral distinction between truth and falsehood, . . . a thorough - going hack-demagogue, coarse, vulgar, and impudent, with a vein of low humor exactly suited to the rabble of a popular city and equally so to the taste of the present House of Representatives." Other similar bits of that pessimism and belief in the deterioration of the times, so common in old men, occasionally appear. In August, 1835, he thinks that " the signs of the times are portentous. All the tendencies of legislation are to the removal of restrictions from the vicious and the guilty, and to the exercise of all the powers of government, legislative, judicial, and executive, by lawless assemblages of individuals." December 27, 1838, he looks upon the Senate and the House, " the cream of the land, the culled darlings of fifteen millions," and observes that " the remarkable phenomenon that they present is the level of intellect and of morals upon which they stand ; and this universal mediocrity is the basis upon which the liberties of this nation repose." In July, 1840, he thinks that

" parties are falling into profligate factions. I have seen this before ; but the worst symptom now is the change in the manners of the people. The continuance of the present Administration . . . will open wide all the flood-gates of corruption. Will a change produce reform? Pause and ponder! Slavery, the Indians, the public lands, the collection and disbursement of public money, the tariff, and foreign affairs: — what is to become of them?"

On January 29, 1841, Henry A. Wise uttered "a motley compound of eloquence and folly, of braggart impudence and childish vanity, of self-laudation and Virginian narrow-mindedness." After him Hubbard, of Alabama, "began grunting against the tariff." Three days later Black, of Georgia, "poured forth his black bile" for an hour and a half. The next week we find Clifford, of Maine, "muddily bothering his trickster invention" to get over a rule of the House, and "snapping like a mackerel at a red rag" at the suggestion of a way to do so. In July, 1841, we again hear of Atherton as a "cross-grained numskull . . . snarling against the loan bill." With such peppery passages in great abundance the Diary is thickly and piquantly besprinkled. They are not always pleasant, perhaps not even always amusing, but they display the marked element of censoriousness in Mr. Adams's character, which it is necessary to appreciate in order to understand some parts of his career.

If Mr. Adams never had the cheerful support of popularity, so neither did he often have the encouragement of success. He said that he was paying in his declining years for the good luck which had attended the earlier portion of his life. On December 14, 1833, he calculates that he has three fourths of the people of Massachusetts against him, and by estranging the anti-Masons he is about to become obnoxious to the whole. " My public life will terminate by the alienation from me of all mankind. . . . It is the experience of all ages that the people grow weary of old men. I cannot flatter myself that I shall escape the common law of our nature." Yet he acknowledges that he is unable to " abstract himself from the great questions which agitate the country." Soon after he again writes in the same vein : " To be forsaken by all mankind seems to be the destiny that awaits my last days." August 6, 1835, he gives as his reason for not accepting an invitation to deliver a discourse, that " instead of having any beneficial influence upon the public mind, it would be turned as an instrument of obloquy against myself." So it had been, as he enumerates, with his exertions against Freemasonry, his labors for internal improvement, for the manufacturing interest, for domestic industry, for free labor, for the disinterested aid then lately brought by him to Jackson in the dispute with France; "so it will be to the end of my political life."

When to unpopularity and reiterated disappointment we add the physical ills of old age, it no longer surprises us to find Mr. Adams at times harsh and bitter beyond the excuse of the occasion. That he was a man of strong physique and of extraordinary powers of endurance, often surpassing those of young and vigorous men, is evident. For example, one day in March, 1840, he notes incidentally: "I walked home and found my family at dinner. From my breakfast yesterday morning until one this afternoon, twenty-eight hours, I had fasted." Many a time he showed like, if not quite equal vigor. But he had been a hard worker all his life, and testing the powers of one's constitution does not tend to their preservation; he was by no means free from the woes of the flesh or from the depression which comes with years and the dread of decrepitude. Already as early as October 7, 1833, he fears that his health is "irretrievable;" he gets but five hours a night of "disturbed unquiet sleep — full of tossings." February 17, 1834, his "voice was so hoarse and feeble that it broke repeatedly, and he could scarcely articulate. It is gone forever," he very mistakenly but despondingly adds, "and it is in vain for me to contend against the decay of time and nature." His enemies found little truth in this foreboding for many sessions thereafter. Only a year after he had performed his feat of fasting for twenty-eight hours of business, he received a letter from a stranger advising him to retire. He admits that perhaps he ought to do so, but says that more than sixty years of public life have made activity necessary to him; it is the "weakness of his nature" which he has "intellect enough left to perceive but not energy to control," so that "the world will retire from me before I shall retire from the world."

The brief sketch which can be given in a volume of this size of so long and so busy a life does not suffice even to indicate all its many industries. The anti-slavery labors of Mr. Adams during his Congressional career were alone an abundant occupation for a man in the prime of life; but to these he added a wonderful list of other toils and interests. He was not only an incessant student in history, politics, and literature, but he also constantly invaded the domain of science. He was Chairman of the Congressional Committee on the Smithsonian bequest, and for several years he gave much time and attention to it, striving to give the fund a direction in favor of science;

he hoped to make it subservient to a plan which
he had long cherished for the building of a
noble national observatory. He had much
committee work; he received many visitors;
he secured hours of leisure for his favorite pursuit of composing poetry; he delivered an enormous number of addresses and speeches upon
all sorts of occasions; he conducted an extensive correspondence; he was a very devout man,
regularly going to church and reading three
chapters in his Bible every day; and he kept
up faithfully his colossal Diary. For several
months in the midst of Congressional duties he
devoted great labor, thought, and anxiety to
the famous cause of the slaves of the Amistad,
in which he was induced to act as counsel before the Supreme Court. Such were the labors
of his declining age. To men of ordinary calibre the multiplicity of his acquirements and
achievements is confounding and incredible.
He worked his brain and his body as unspar-
ingly as if they had been machines insensible to
the pleasure or necessity of rest. Surprisingly
did they submit to his exacting treatment, last-
ing in good order and condition far beyond
what was then the average of life and vigorous
faculties among his contemporaries engaged in
public affairs.

In August, 1842, while he was still tarrying

in the unwholesome heats of Washington, he
had some symptoms which he thought premoni-
itory, and he speaks of the next session of Congress as probably the last which he should ever
attend. March 25, 1844, he gives a painful
sketch of himself. Physical disability, he says,
must soon put a stop to his Diary. That morning he had risen " at four, and with smarting,
bloodshot eyes and shivering hand, still sat down
and wrote to fill up the chasm of the closing
days of last week." If his remaining days were
to be few he was at least resolved to make them
long for purposes of unremitted labor.

But he had one great joy and distinguished
triumph still in store for him. From the time
when the " gag " rule had been first established,
Mr. Adams had kept up an unbroken series of
attacks upon it at all times and by all means.
At the beginning of the several sessions, when
the rules were established by the House, he
always moved to strike out this one. Year
after year his motion was voted down, but year
after year he renewed it with invincible perseverance. The majorities against him began
to dwindle till they became almost impercep-
tible; in 1842 it was a majority of four; in
1843, of three; in 1844 the struggle was protracted for weeks, and Mr. Adams all but carried the day. It was evident that victory was

not far off, and a kind fate had destined him to
live not only to see but himself to win it.   On
December 3, 1844, he made his usual motion
and called for the yeas and nays ; a motion was
made to lay his motion on the table, and upon
that also the question was taken by yeas and
nays — eighty-one yeas, one hundred and four
nays, and his motion was *not* laid on the table.
The question was then put upon it, and it was
carried by the handsome vote of one hundred
and eight to eighty.   In that moment the
" gag " rule became a thing of the past, and
Mr. Adams had conquered in his last fight.
" Blessed, forever blessed, be the name of God ! "
he writes in recording the event.   A week
afterwards some anti-slavery petitions were received and actually referred to the Committee
on the District of Columbia.   This glorious consummation having been achieved, this advanced
stage in the long conflict having been reached,
Mr. Adams could not hope for life to see another goal passed.   His work was nearly done ;
he had grown aged, and had worn himself out
faithfully toiling in the struggle which must
hereafter be fought through its coming phases
and to its final success by others, younger men
than he, though none of them certainly having
over him any other militant advantage save
only the accident of youth.

His mental powers were not less than at any
time in the past when, on November 19, 1846,
he was struck by paralysis in the street in Boston. He recovered from the attack, however,
sufficiently to resume his duties in Washington
some three months later. His reappearance in
the House was marked by a pleasing incident :
all the members rose together ; business was for
the moment suspended ; his old accustomed seat
was at once surrendered to him by the gentleman
to whom it had fallen in the allotment, and he
was formally conducted to it by two members.
After this, though punctual in attendance, he
only once took part in debate. On February
21, 1848, he appeared in his seat as usual. At
half past one in the afternoon the Speaker was
rising to put a question, when he was suddenly
interrupted by cries of " Stop ! Stop ! — Mr.
Adams ! " Some gentlemen near Mr. Adams
had thought that he was striving to rise to address the Speaker, when in an instant he fell
over insensible. The members thronged around
him in great confusion. The House hastily adjourned. He was placed on a sofa and removed
first to the hall of the rotunda and then to the
Speaker's room. Medical men were in attendance but could be of no service in the presence
of death. The stern old fighter lay dying almost
on the very field of so many battles and in the

very tracks in which he had so often stood erect and unconquerable, taking and dealing so many mighty blows. Late in the afternoon some inarticulate mutterings were construed into the words, "Thank the officers of the House." Soon again he said intelligibly, "This is the last of earth! I am content!" It was his extreme utterance. He lay thereafter unconscious till the evening of the 23d, when he passed quietly away.

He lies buried "under the portal of the church at Quincy" beside his wife, who survived him four years, his father and his mother. The memorial tablet inside the church bears upon it the words "Alteri Sæculo," — surely never more justly or appropriately applied to any man than to John Quincy Adams, hardly abused and cruelly misappreciated in his own day but whom subsequent generations already begin to honor as one of the greatest of American statesmen, not only preëminent in ability and acquirements, but even more to be honored for profound, immutable honesty of purpose and broad, noble humanity of aims.

INDEX

INDEX

at St. Petersburg, 70, 71 ; his success as foreign representative, 71, 72 ; disgusted by snobbery of American travelers, 72 ; declines to take part in squabbles for precedence, 72, 73 ; hampered by meagre salary, 73 ; describes Russia during Napoleonic wars, 74 ; nominated to act as peace commissioner with England, 75, 76 ; describes negotiations in his diary, 77 ; suggests refusing to meet British commissioners at their lodgings, 77 ; remarks on arrogance of British, 81 ; vents irritation upon colleagues, 82, 83 ; begins drafting communications, but abandons duty to Gallatin, 82 ; nettled at criticisms of colleagues on his drafts, 82, 83 ; quarrels with all but Gallatin, 84 ; incompatible with Clay, 84 ; urges strong counter-claims, 85 ; thinks negotiations certain to fail, 86 ; obliged to work for peace as defeated party, 86, 87 ; willing to return to *status quo*, 87 ; disagrees with Clay over fisheries and Mississippi navigation, 88 ; determined to insist on fisheries, 89, 90, 92 ; suspects British intend to prevent peace, 90 ; controverts Goulburn, 91 ; signs treaty, 93 ; at Paris during Napoleon's "hundred days," 98 ; appointed Minister to England, 98 ; with Clay and Gallatin, makes treaty of commerce with England, 98 ; his slight duties as minister, 98, 99 ; bored by English dinners, 99, 100 ; sensitive to small income, 100.

Secretary of State. Appointed, 100 ; describes dullness of Washington in diary, 102 ; as host, 103 ; his habits of life, 104 ; prominent candidate for succession to Monroe, 105 ; intrigued against by Crawford, 106 ; and by Clay and Calhoun, 106, 107 ; expects Spanish colonies to gain independence,

109 ; but maintains cautious public attitude, 109 ; describes Spanish ambassador, 111 ; negotiates concerning boundaries of Louisiana, 111, 112 ; his position, 112 ; fears opposition from Clay and Crawford, 112 ; urged by Monroe not to claim too much, 113 ; rejects English mediation, 114 ; uses French Minister as go-between, 114 ; succeeds in reaching a conclusion, 114, 115 ; a triumph for his diplomacy, 115 ; chagrined at discovery of Spanish land grants, 116, 117 ; and at refusal of Spanish government to ratify treaty, 118 ; urges the seizure of disputed territory, 118 ; at first indifferent to Missouri question, 119 ; soon appreciates the slavery issue, 119 ; predicts an attempt to dissolve the Union, 119, 120 ; sharp comments on slavery, slaveholders, and Northern weakness, 120 ; notes Calhoun's threat of alliance of slave States with England, 121 ; thinks abolition impossible without disunion, 121, 122 ; maintains power of Congress over slavery in Territories, 122 ; realizes that failure of treaty damages his chance for presidency, 123 ; refuses to reopen question with new Spanish envoy, 123 ; forces ratification of treaty with annulment of land grants, 124 ; his satisfaction with outcome of negotiations, 125, 126 ; prepares report on weights and measures, 126 ; its thoroughness, 127 ; his pride of country without boastfulness in negotiations, 127, 128 ; declines to consider what European courts may think, 128, 129 ; considers it destiny of United States to occupy North America, 129 ; considers annexation of Cuba probable, 130 ; always willing to encroach within America, 130, 131 ; tells Russia American

petition for removal of Adams to be a hoax, 280.

Hamilton, Alexander, real leader of Federalist party during John Adams's administration, 27; his feud with Adams, 27; his influence in Massachusetts, 28, 30.

Harvard College, studies of John Quincy Adams in, 17; its proposal to confer degree upon Jackson opposed by Adams, 241 ; confers the degree, 241, 242.

Haynes, Charles E., moves rejection of Adams's petition from slaves, 270, 275 ; moves to make censure of Adams severe, 271.

Hayti, its possible representation at Panama Congress causes South to advocate refusal to send delegates, 191 ; petitions for recognition of, 259.

Holland, mission of Adams to, 20 ; conquered by France, 20; made into "Batavian Republic," 20 ; agrees to suppress slave trade, 138.

Holy Alliance, fear of its attempting to reconquer Spanish colonies, 132, 134, 136.

House of Representatives, Adams's career in, 225–308 ; election of Adams to, 225 ; his labors in committee and other work of, 227; solitariness of Adams in, 231; his position in, with regard to tariff of 1833, 235; debate in, over Jackson's policy to France, 239 ; anti-slavery petitions presented in, at first without remark, 243, 248 ; debates plans to prevent their reception, 248–250 ; adopts "gag" rule against Adams's protest, 251; attempts of Adams to infringe its rule, 257, 258 ; debates power to abolish slavery, 262 ; debates proposed censure of Adams for presenting a petition from slaves, 269–279 ; resolves that slaves do not possess right of petition, 279 ; Adams's speech in reply, 277–279 ; attempts to censure Adams for presenting petition for dissolution of Union, 280–288 ; lays subject on table, 288 ; does not resent a second disunion petition, 288 ; refusal of Garland to organize according to custom, in 1839, 290–292 ; appeals to Adams, 292 ; organized by his leadership, 293–295 ; pays compliment to Adams on his return after illness, 307; death of Adams in, 307, 308.

Hubbard, David, comment of Adams on, 300.

Hunter, R. M. T., elected Speaker of House, 295.

Impressment, description of its exercise by England and effects upon United States, 43–45; difficulty of reclaiming impressed Americans, 44, 45; the Chesapeake affair, 45, 46 ; not mentioned in treaty of Ghent, 92, 95; later negotiations over, 99.

Indians, propositions concerning, in peace negotiations, 78; dissensions over, between American commissioners, 90; article concerning, 94.

Internal improvements, Adams's advocacy of, 194, 201.

Jackson, Andrew, his view of Adams's office-seeking, 63 ; wins battle of New Orleans, 96, 97 ; his outrages in Spanish territory, 110 ; enrages Spain, 111 ; approves Adams's Spanish treaty, later condemns it, 125 ; becomes candidate for presidency in 1824, 149 ; his Indian wars in Florida, 158, 159 ; hangs Arbuthnot and Ambrister, 159 ; captures Pensacola, 159; difficulty of praising or blaming him, 159, 160 ; condemned by President and Cabinet, 160 ; and by Clay, 160 ; defended by Adams, 160–162 ; ball in his honor given by Adams, 162 ; supported for Minister to Mexico and for

of, during debate over Texas annexation, 243.

Senate of the United States, election of Adams to, 30 ; unpopularity of Adams in, 31–33 ; rejects all his proposals, 31, 32 ; debates acquisition of Louisiana, 35 ; impeaches Chase, 36 ; increased influence of Adams in, 36, 37 ; adopts Adams's resolutions demanding indemnity for British seizures, 39 ; his career in, reviewed by Adams, 66–68 ; refuses, then accepts, Adams's nomination as Minister to Russia, 69, 70 ; rejects Gallatin's nomination as peace commissioner, 75.

Seward, W. H., on John Adams's recall of J. Q. Adams before end of term, 25 ; on Adams's dissatisfaction with election of 1824, 174.

Shakespeare, Adams's opinion of, 222.

Slaveholders in Congress, their hatred of Adams, 229, 246 ; attacked by Adams, 258, 259 ; outwitted by Adams, 261, 273 ; condemn Adams for arguing possibility of abolition under war power, 262, 264 ; enraged at Adams's having a petition from slaves, 269, 270 ; move to censure him, 271 ; discomfited by discovery of nature of petition, 273 ; renew attempt to censure, 274, 275 ; abandon it, 276, 279 ; bitterly attacked by Adams in his defense, 277–279 ; try to censure Adams for presenting disunion petition, 281–283 ; defied by Adams, 283–285 ; threaten Adams with assassination, 286, 287 ; abandon attempt, 287, 288 ; refuse to serve on committee with Adams, 289 ; respect his courage, 290 ; applaud his energy in carrying out organization of House, 293, 294.

Slavery, strengthened by Louisiana purchase, 35 ; made a politi-

cal issue by Missouri question, 119 ; opinions of Adams concerning, 119–121 ; extension of, opposed by Adams, 121 ; formation of a party devoted to, 188–192 ; attack upon, hastened by Texas question, 243 ; Adams's part in war against, 244–248 ; right of Congress to abolish, under war power, 250, 261–265.

Slaves, English seizures of, during war of 1812, negotiations concerning, 99.

Slave trade, refusal of Adams to submit United States to mixed tribunals for its repression, 135–137 ; English proposal for combined effort, 137, 138.

Smith, William, accuses Adams of monomania, 280.

Smithsonian bequest, connection of Adams with, 303.

South, the, Calhoun its leader in 1824, 149 ; does not support Adams for President, 169, 183 ; begins to form a new slavery party in Adams's administration, 188, 189 ; opposes Panama Congress because of Hayti's share in it, 191.

Southard, Samuel L., reappointed Secretary of Navy, 177.

South Carolina, refusal of Adams to placate, in 1828, 201 ; protests against tariff, 233 ; its punishment for nullification desired by Adams, 234–237 ; Jackson's vacillation toward, condemned by Adams, 234–236 ; gains its point from Clay, 236.

Spain, danger of war with, in Monroe's administration, 108 ; question of revolted colonies, 108, 109 ; disputes over Louisiana boundary and Florida, 109, 110 ; sends Onis to negotiate, 111 ; its policy hampers Onis, 111, 112 ; negotiations, 113–116 ; repudiates Onis's treaty, 117 ; accepts original treaty, 124 ; agrees to suppress slave trade,

138; angered at Jackson's excesses in Florida, 161.

Spanish - American republics, wish aid from United States, 108; frowned down by European countries, 108; sympathy for, in United States, 108, 109; recognition urged by Clay, 109, 152; recognized gradually, 132 : danger of attempt to reconquer by Holy Alliance, 132, 133; protected by Monroe doctrine, 131-134.

Sterret, ——, his removal urged by Clay for planning an insult to Adams, 179; not removed by Adams, 180.

TARIFF, Adams's views upon, 234; compromise tariff of 1833, considered by Adams a surrender, 235.

Tennessee, renominates Jackson for President, 181; repeats bargain story, 183.

Texas, proposal to annex, arouses Northern opposition to slavery, 243; indignation of Adams at, 265, 266; held by Adams to be unconstitutional, 266.

Thaxter, ——, teacher of Adams, 3.

Thompson, Waddy, sarcastic remark of, 259; neglects to present petition for Adams's expulsion, 268; introduces resolution of censure upon Adams, 271; threatens Adams with criminal proceedings, 271; presents new resolutions, 274; scored by Adams, 277.

Tompkins, Daniel D., candidate for President in 1824, 149.

Times, London, condemns treaty of Ghent, 97.

Tracy, Uriah, supports Adams in Senate, 68.

Treaty of Ghent, meeting of commissioners, 76; irritation during negotiations, 77; preliminary conflict as to place of meeting, 77, 78; large demands of England for cession of territory and other advantages, 78, 79; discussion

over proposed belt of neutral Indian territory, 79; and of demand for Mississippi navigation, 80; complaints by Americans of manners of English, 80-82; bickerings among Americans, 81-84; difficulties in drafting documents, 82, 83; social intercourse between commissioners, 85, 92; expected failure of negotiations, 86; *status ante bellum* proposed by Adams, 87; sanctioned by United States, 87; dissensions among commissioners over Mississippi navigation and fisheries, 88-90; over Moose Island, 91; English offer to omit fisheries and Mississippi, 92; abandonment of impressment article by Americans, 92; peculiarities of negotiation, 93; alteration of English policy, 93; terms of treaty, 94; a success for Americans, 95, 96; rejoicings over, in America, 96; condemned in England, 97.

Trimble, Cary A., of Ohio, opposes Spanish treaty, 124.

Tuyl, Baron, discussion of Adams with, concerning Alaska, 131.

VAN BUREN, MARTIN, becomes manager of Jackson's followers, 192; compared by Adams to Burr, 193.

Vanderpoel, Aaron, tries to prevent Adams from replying to resolutions of censure by previous question, 276.

Virginia, refusal of Adams to placate, in election of 1828, 201.

Vivès, General, supplants Onis, 123; Adams's stubborn attitude toward, 123, 124; forced to yield, 124.

Von Holst, H. C., calls Adams last of the statesmen to be President, 213.

WAR OF 1812, a defeat for United States, 76, 86.

War power of Congress, held by

The Riverside Press

CAMBRIDGE, MASSACHUSETTS, U. S. A.
ELECTROTYPED AND PRINTED BY
H. O. HOUGHTON AND CO.